BACK TO BOKHARA

By the same author

EASTERN APPROACHES

DISPUTED BARRICADE

A PERSON FROM ENGLAND

BACK
TO BOKHARA

FITZROY MACLEAN

JONATHAN CAPE
THIRTY BEDFORD SQUARE
LONDON

PRINTED IN GREAT BRITAIN IN THE CITY OF OXFORD
AT THE ALDEN PRESS
ON PAPER MADE BY JOHN DICKINSON & CO.
COLLOTYPE ILLUSTRATIONS BY L. VAN LEER & CO., N.V.,
AMSTERDAM
BOUND BY A. W. BAIN & CO. LTD, LONDON

CONTENTS

ILLUSTRATIONS

ACKNOWLEDGMENTS

My thanks and acknowledgments are due to the *Sunday Times* for their kindness and generosity in connection with this journey; to *Life* Magazine for permission to reproduce the photograph of Mr Khrushchov and myself opposite page 116; and to my secretary, Miss Jeanne Thomlinson, for her help in preparing the text.

For Susan Rose and Jeremy

BACK TO BOKHARA

ONE

TWENTY YEARS AFTER

THERE is, I think, something intrinsically fascinating in the idea of returning after a prolonged interval to a country in which you have once spent several months or years of your life and which you have not revisited since. All the more so when the impression left behind by that country has been a strong one and the time spent there of importance in one way or another to your development. What changes, you wonder, will you find in the places to which you are returning? What changes, for that matter, in yourself, in your attitude to life, in your capacity for observation and comprehension?

From time to time during the twenty years which had passed since I had last seen the Soviet Union, I had felt a certain curiosity to go back. But for a variety of reasons it was not until last summer that the project seriously took shape. Having once taken shape it materialized fairly swiftly. Some articles were planned and commissioned. A Soviet visa was applied for and, after an interval, granted. Reservations were booked and a provisional itinerary made out.

During the two years I had spent in the Soviet Union before the War I had managed by one means or another to penetrate to the remoter parts of Russian Turkestan, to the foothills of the Tien Shan and the borders of Sinkiang, to Tashkent, Samarkand and Bokhara, at that time all officially closed to foreigners. Now, once again, I was anxious to return there. 'If you wish to go to Turkestan you will have to travel de luxe,' said the charming blonde young lady at the Soviet Embassy to whom I explained my aims. 'Nothing,' I replied, 'could suit me better.' And so it was as a tourist de luxe under the auspices of Intourist, the Soviet State Tourist Agency, that I set out on my return visit to the Soviet Union, ultimately bound, or so I very much hoped, for the legendary cities of Turkestan.

In trying to form an estimate of what is happening in the Soviet Union nothing is more necessary than a standard of comparison, a criterion by which to judge what you see there. So deep is the gulf set between the capitalist and communist worlds, so alien is everything Soviet to ordinary Western conceptions, so radically different are the basic assumptions on which Soviet thought is based, so great and so sudden the contrasts and the extremes, that without such a criterion the visitor will very quickly become bewildered. It is like finding oneself suddenly translated to another planet.

In this respect I was lucky. During the two years I had spent in Russia before the War I had, in the course of my duties at the Embassy, made a fairly close study of various aspects of Soviet life and Soviet policy. And so, returning now after an absence of almost exactly twenty years, I had a ready-made standard of comparison: I could compare the Soviet Union of 1958 with the Soviet Union of 1938. The years I had spent in Moscow — 1937, 1938 and the beginning of 1939 — were the years when Stalinism in a sense reached its culmination. Stalin himself had long since won his battle over his real or imagined opponents. With the exaggerated thoroughness of a homicidal maniac he was next making sure that no vestige of opposition should ever emerge again. The purges were at their height. Millions of people were being imprisoned or shot on the flimsiest pretexts or on no pretext at all. Terror was rife. You could see it in the people's faces in the street. The whole population lived in fear of the dreaded knock on the door at three o'clock in the morning. The secret police were ubiquitous. Suspicion hung over everything and seeped in everywhere like a poisonous mist. No one trusted anyone else. Contact with foreigners, even foreign Communists, was the most dangerous thing of all — a veritable kiss of death, to be shunned like the plague. For the foreigner living in Moscow the hardest thing in the world was to meet, to talk to, to get to know a Soviet citizen. The regime subsisted in a meticulously preserved vacuum, carefully guarded against all danger of contamination from the outside world.

Against this background Stalin was bludgeoning through his programme. The collectivization of agriculture had already been ruthlessly enforced at a tremendous cost in human lives and suffering. Now, by a succession of Five Year Plans, the country, backward as it was, was being massively industrialized. Everything was sacrificed to the Moloch of Heavy Industry — first and foremost the standard of living of the people. The population was badly fed and badly clothed. The few consumer goods available in the shops were in short supply and of pathetically poor quality. Housing conditions were appalling and little or nothing was being done to improve them. Heavy industry came first.

And so the impression I took away after two years had been one of fear, misery, squalor and the total suppression of all freedom. And yet it was impossible not to be attracted by the country and the people. Impossible not to be aware of their qualities, of their dynamism, of their tremendous potential energies and resources. Impossible, too, not to want to know where all this was leading, what the ultimate outcome of this gigantic and seemingly unnatural social, political and economic experiment would be.

Would it end, as it had begun, in an explosion of violence and bloodshed? Would it founder and collapse in a morass of inefficiency and bureaucratic muddle? Was it, or was it not, conceivable that it might succeed? Or might it, perhaps, gradually transform itself into something completely different? What, finally, would be the effect of the eventual, the inevitable disappearance of the man on whose shoulders the whole structure rested, who had battered it into shape and given it its grim mono-lithic character, of Josif Vissarionovich Stalin, in whose hands were gathered all the reins of power?

The evening paper I bought at London Airport carried in banner headlines the news of the launching by the Russians of a third Sputnik. As I sipped a glass of acquavit and settled down to the delicious dinner and no less excellent bottle of Burgundy provided by Scandina-vian Air Services, I turned over in my mind this timely reminder that in one way and another things had changed in the Soviet Union since before the War. Then, the view held by most foreigners was that the Russians were barely capable of constructing a sparking-plug, let alone anything more complicated. Now, this was quite manifestly not the case.

I was still in a reflective mood next day when, after a night spent in Stockholm, I looked up from my pre-luncheon glass of acquavit to find that having crossed the Baltic we were approaching the Gulf of Riga with the farms and pine forests of Latvia spreading away beyond its blue waters. A couple of minutes later we had crossed the coast and were flying over what I suddenly realized was Soviet territory.

Here was another change. Since my last visit the Soviet Union had increased in size. The country that I had known as Latvia had ceased to exist. In 1940, while most of us were preoccupied elsewhere, it had been eaten up. It had become a part of the Soviet Union. And so had Esthonia and Lithuania. I had motored home from Moscow through the Baltic States in the spring of 1939 — their last year of independence, as it turned out — and I remembered what nice little countries they had been: clean, tidy, orderly and prosperous. What, I wondered, were they like now? What had become, under communism, of Riga, of those neat rows of houses, of those well-stocked shops, of the pleasant hotel where I had stayed and the agreeable little night-club adjoining it, of those thousands of well-conducted, respectable-looking citizens — *bons bourgeois* in the fullest sense of the word?

But soon our aircraft had left behind what was now the

Soviet Socialist Republic of Latvia and was flying over a region of immense forests. Here and there in the clearings one could see little clusters of wooden *isbas* with smoke rising from their chimneys and tracks leading to the village well. This was Russia proper, the Russia I knew. It seemed strange to be entering it in anything but a Soviet conveyance; strange to be flying over it in anything so completely non-Russian as this intensely Western, intensely Scandinavian aeroplane, with its acquavit and smörgasbord, its trim ash-blonde Scandinavian air-hostess and equally trim, equally Scandinavian air-crew. And I remembered how, when I had travelled out to Moscow before the War, we had had to leave our International Sleeping Car with its familiar brown-uniformed conductor and its blue monogrammed china at the Soviet frontier station, and had there transferred ourselves and our luggage to an unfamiliar Soviet sleeping-car with a Soviet conductor and a samovar, while the coach we had travelled in was summarily shunted back the way it had come, as though infected with the plague.

This time the transition was in one way less abrupt, in another more so. Here I was already over Soviet territory and in Soviet air space, and yet, so to speak, still in a tiny Scandinavian enclave, still eating Scandinavian food and still surrounded by Scandinavians. It was a modern phenomenon that one did not notice travelling to other countries. There was, for instance, nothing particularly odd about landing in Turkey or Japan in a British aeroplane. But the Soviet Union, somehow, was different. We were travelling, after all, not just to another country or continent, but to another world.

The forests lasted most of the way to Moscow, with here and there stretches of pasture and cultivation and small towns and straggling villages. Then all of a sudden, as we began to circle and descend, I saw the skyscrapers, ten or twenty miles away across the plain — a whole row of fantastic towers and spires where before there had been nothing. It was only a glimpse, and then we were taxiing over the tarmac to an airport which looked, and was, very much like any other airport.

On stepping out of the aeroplane I was greeted with an invitation to a party — a cocktail party at the British Embassy, to meet the members of the English and Soviet football teams who were to play each other in the Dynamo Stadium in two days' time. Would I like to come straight to the party, Patrick Reilly had written on the back of this invitation. I could think of nothing I should like better, and so, stepping delightedly into the car which he had most hospitably sent to meet me, I was soon driving at a steady sixty miles an hour along the great new arterial road which leads into Moscow from the airport.

Before very long we had come to the outskirts of the town — new outskirts and, it seemed to me at first sight, very largely a new town: block upon massive block of brand-new flats, square, unornamented, ten or fifteen storeys high, some recently completed, others still being built, with cranes swinging to and fro and builders clambering about on ladders or perilously poised on cradles. Row upon row of them, reaching along both sides of the road and radiating away at right-angles into the remote distance.

Here and there, as we approached the centre of the town, I began to recognize an occasional street or an occasional building which for some reason or other I happened to recall, for the most part typical old pre-revolutionary Russian houses of green, blue, red or yellow and white stucco. But for every building I remembered there were two or three entirely new ones — shops, blocks of flats, office blocks, institutes or institutions — with, every now and then, round a corner or at the end of a street, a sudden surprising glimpse of an enormous, a fantastic skyscraper — a high house, as the Russians call them, a *visotny dom* — preposterous, portentous, in what had been essentially a town of low, cosy, rather modest little houses. There could be no doubt about it. From a straggling, overgrown provincial town, Moscow since I had last seen it had become a great city. A city completely unlike London or Rome or Paris or New York, but a great city all the same, and, what is more, one that in a rough and ready way was growing as you watched it.

And then all of a sudden we came out on to the banks of the Moscow River, and there, opposite us in the bright sunlight, perched high on its eminence above the fast-flowing muddy stream, more fantastic than I had remembered, more fantastic than any skyscraper, was the Kremlin, with its conglomeration of turrets and spires, of churches and palaces, of domes and pinnacles, of glittering gold and stucco and stone and rose-red brick, all contained and encompassed by the towers and battlements and gates

22

of its great surrounding wall. It was a spectacle that I had lived opposite to day in, day out for two years, but a spectacle which, by its strangeness, its secrecy, its barbaric splendour, still took me by surprise and, I suspected, always would take me by surprise.

As we drove into the Embassy forecourt the Soviet militiamen on duty oustide the gate saluted, and I noticed with pleasure that they no longer wore their former dreary greenish-grey tunics, but were now clad in handsome scarlet and blue uniforms adorned with a profusion of shining buttons which gave them the appearance of Ruritanian generals. The Embassy, on the other hand, was exactly as I remembered it. There was no mistaking that wedding-cake exterior, that lavish jumble of styles within. Stalin, it seemed, glowering balefully out across the river from the Kremlin, had finally decided to take it away and make a park there. But, as it happened he had died before the project could be carried out. And so, at the time of writing, Her Majesty's Ambassador is still housed in his massive yellow palace, once the mansion of a sugar millionaire.

The party for the footballers was already in full swing when I arrived, and although the footballers themselves, being in training for Saturday's match, could neither eat nor drink, a good time was clearly being had by all. But to me perhaps the most remarkable thing about this pleasant function was the large number of Russians who were there and, what was more, were talking away unconcernedly to all and sundry. This was something completely new in my experience, and something that gave me reason to hope that I might on this visit at last be able to do something that I had always wanted to do and had so far never been able to do — namely talk freely and unrestrictedly to any Soviet citizens I might fall in with. If this was really so, here was an enormous difference straight away.

But by now it was getting late and it occurred to me that I had better make sure of a room for the night.

Having previously always lived in my own flat, I had never before stayed in a hotel in Moscow. But my recollection was that the National Hotel, just opposite the back-door of the Kremlin, was rather a nice one — old-fashioned but not exaggeratedly so, a kind of Russian Ritz. Lenin, it appeared, had always stayed there during the later stages of the Revolution, which in itself gave it a certain cachet. I also knew it to be the headquarters of Intourist with whom inevitably I should have a good deal to do during my stay in Moscow. And so, from London, I had booked myself a room there.

The National was all that I remembered it to be. The coffered ceiling of the slightly fusty entrance hall was supported by four massive marble caryatides. The staircase had a stair-rail of heavily wrought iron and highly polished brass. The young lady sitting at the reception desk under a gigantic portrait of Lenin was both attractive and friendly. But she had not got a room for me. No, she said wistfully but firmly, after referring the matter to higher authority, I had been booked in at the Ukraina and to the Ukraina I must go. A car would take me there at once. 'What,' I asked, 'is the Ukraina like?' 'Just wait till you see it,' she replied excitedly. 'It is only a year old. It is our very latest hotel.'

After a headlong drive to the outskirts of the city, the Intourist car finally deposited me on the doorstep of the Hotel Ukraina and then drove smartly away. Glancing nervously upwards, I found that I was standing at the foot of a medium-sized skyscraper. Some thirty storeys towered sheerly above me like a cliff; twin wings, a mere twenty storeys high, loomed to left and right. A porch as big as a good-sized house stood in front of me. Feeling a little giddy I pushed my way through the immense swing doors and found myself in an entrance hall the size of Waterloo Station, filled with a seething, shouting crowd of people of all sizes, ages, sexes and nationalities.

At the far side was a reception desk. Here the crowd was thicker than ever. Elbowing my way through it I eventually succeeded in attracting the attention of one of several large, middle-aged, motherly-looking women who were sitting on the other side, and she, after surprisingly few preliminaries, thrust a key into my hand and then turned good-naturedly to the frantic Chinese who was next to me in the queue.

Having obtained my key, the next thing was to find my room. This was easier said than done. There are no stairs in the Ukraina. And not all lifts go to all floors. The lifts, moreover, which are operated by personable but impatient young women and are always crammed full, only run at fixed intervals, like trains on the Inner Circle, and are easy neither to get into nor to get out of. Having stepped a trifle impetuously into the wrong lift, been carried to the wrong floor, got out, caught another lift

back to the ground floor, got into the right lift, discovered
that the room to which I had been given a key was already
very much occupied by three unidentifiable foreigners,
caught another lift full of what seemed to be West
Africans back to the ground floor, fought my way back to
the reception desk, made a fuss, got another key and then
another lift, found my real room, a square white boxlike
affair on the fifteenth floor with a glittering bathroom
attached, deposited my luggage there and finally caught a
downward-bound lift back to the ground floor, I was not
surprised to find that it was nearly midnight.

By now I was extremely hungry, and the great white
dining-room with its rows of expectant waiters and shining
cutlery and glass looked exactly what I wanted. The only
trouble was that it seemed to be shut. I rattled at the glass
door. Dinner, they came and told me, is only being served
to delegations. But this did not deter me. I am, I said
without a moment's hesitation, the British Delegation,
and five minutes later under the shadow of a small individual Union Jack, and I am afraid, under slightly false
pretences, I was drinking a badly needed tot of vodka and
eating my way through the first course of an extremely
good dinner: caviar, *shashlik*, and an excellent bottle of
red wine from the Caucasus.

Meanwhile, all round me, the delegations were flocking in to feed: black and white, brown and yellow,
African, European, Asian, American, men and women,
some serious, some uproarious, some bored and sullen,
others as keen as mustard, some accompanied by Russians,
others on their own, some painfully sober, some slightly
drunk. What they were all delegated to, and by whom, I

26

never discovered. But these were only a beginning. For the rest of my stay in the Soviet Union, wherever I went, hotels, trains, aeroplanes were all swarming with delegates.

The importance of these innumerable delegates and delegations only dawned on me gradually. Before the War even a dedicated Communist like Tito could see for himself that there was something badly the matter with the Soviet Union. The terror, the squalor, the misery, the muddle were manifest. But now this was no longer so to anything like the same extent. Swept rapidly from city to city and from republic to republic in a succession of shiny motor cars and jet aeroplanes; installed in immense new hotels; made much of, conducted round model factories and farms and power stations and stadiums and hospitals and universities; greeted everywhere by affable notabilities; overwhelmed with floral tributes and with lavish hospitality, visitors from less advanced countries, from Asia and Africa in particular, could scarcely fail to be impressed by their experiences — in fact might easily come to the conclusion that here lay the future for their own countries and for the whole world. Delegations clearly constituted an extremely important aspect of Soviet foreign policy.

After dinner, feeling the need for some fresh air, I strolled out of the great entrance portico and across the river in the direction of central Moscow. There had been a thunderstorm and the air was cooler. The streets at this hour were quite empty. A solitary cat disappeared round the corner of an immense block of flats. In every window I passed there was, I noticed, a green plant of some kind, usually an aspidistra. The Russians love plants and manage to grow them under the most unpromising conditions.

It was not until the small hours that after another struggle with the lifts, which run less and less frequently as the night wears on, I finally got to bed in my little white room on the fifteenth floor. No sooner had I switched off the semi-compulsory wireless and turned out the light than the telephone rang. 'Teresa!' cried a frenzied male Italian voice, 'Teresa!' Propping myself reluctantly on my elbow, I grunted non-committally. 'Che fai tu dalla Teresa?' asked the voice more frantically than ever: 'What are you doing in Teresa's room?' 'Questo,' I replied with dignity, 'è una cosa che non ti riguarda.' — 'That is nothing to do with you.' And having thus, I hoped, flung a spanner into the intimate life of at least one delegation, I disconnected the telephone and fell dreamlessly asleep.

I would not have missed my night at the Ukraina for anything in the world. But, as I sat at breakfast next morning, eating black bread and red caviar and listening to a French delegate at the next table dictating his first impressions of the Soviet Union into a tape-recorder in the peculiarly articulate French which Frenchmen, especially progressive Frenchmen, employ on such occasions, I knew that I had got to get out of here. In some respects the Ukraina was fine. The food was good. The architecture was impressive. The rooms were clean and bright and airy. The plumbing was faultless. But it was too big and too far away. And the lifts and the delegations would, I knew, end by driving me insane.

And so, after first wheedling my passport out of the reception desk, I hoisted my bags into a taxi and lit out for the National. When I got there the friendly blonde of the day before was still on duty. And now, miraculously, a room was free — indeed more than a room, a whole suite: bedroom, drawing-room and bathroom. I could move in straight away. Handing my bags to a courtly old porter with a gold band round his hat, I moved. This, I sensed, was much more my line than the Ukraina.

My private drawing-room was richly equipped with heavy Empire mahogany furniture. From the ceiling hung an immense gilt chandelier. The windows were draped with heavy green plush curtains and in each corner of the room tall plush-covered columns supported splendid bronze and gilt urns. The floor was covered by a vast Aubusson-type carpet. Scattered freely about the room was a profusion of solidly constructed sofas, tables, chairs, gilt looking-glasses and cut-glass carafes. On the mahogany desk stood an enormous Sèvres-and-ormolu lamp with a heavily fringed shade of pink silk. The inkstand, which was in the manner of Fabergé, was of green marble and polished brass. My bedroom, with its great Empire mahogany bed, was in the same style. The bathroom, though slightly less streamlined than that which I had occupied at the Ukraina, served its purpose equally well.

The decorations in the hotel restaurant matched those in my apartment. The flowered china and heavy cut glass, though products of a present-day Soviet factory, were richly Edwardian in style. Looking round me, I noticed with relief that there were comparatively few delegations;

some Belgians, a small group of East Germans and that was all. The rest of the customers were mainly Russians: some smart and sophisticated (pretty, well-dressed girls, escorted by knowing-looking men); others nondescript in a dull bureaucratic kind of way; a few genuinely proletarian in their working clothes; but all, presumably, well enough supplied with cash or the equivalent to pay the startlingly steep bill with which the waiter in his smart white coat and black bow-tie presented you at the end of your meal.

But the great advantage of the National from my point of view was that it was right in the middle of everything. For a visitor to Moscow there is no more rewarding pastime than simply to walk about the streets looking at people, looking at things, strolling through public gardens and amusement parks, drifting into shops and offices and cinemas and churches and exhibitions and anywhere else where you can gain admittance. Even if you don't speak Russian, and so can't talk to people and ask them questions, you will learn more about the Soviet Union and its inhabitants in this way than by reading every book that has ever been written on the subject. And so, strolling out of the National Hotel I set out to pick up the threads of twenty years ago. 'Chewing gum?' said a little boy hopefully the moment I stepped into the street. Already this was something quite new.

What I now saw at my leisure confirmed my first hurried impressions. Moscow was externally a much more impressive-looking place than it had been. Twenty years ago most of the buildings had seemed either half put up or half pulled down and had a way of staying in that indeterminate condition for months and years on end. Now, as I had already seen on my way in from the airport, whole new districts were springing up on the outskirts where before there had been nothing but mud and desolation. In the centre of the city, too, the streets of little low old-fashioned stucco houses were fast being swept away to make way for more imposing edifices — more imposing but not necessarily more solidly constructed, for some of them were already showing signs of dilapidation. But the general impression was of a great modern city; and the general impression is what the Russians — with their *shirokaya natura* — their wide nature — mind about most.

And then there were the skyscrapers. As soon as he heard that this was not my first visit to the Soviet Union, every Russian I met (and in the course of a week I talked to more Russians than I had met in a year before the War) wanted to know what my impressions were. Did I, they would ask, with engaging anxiety to be told I did, notice many changes? Yes, I would at once reply, thinking I was on safe ground: the skyscrapers, the 'high houses'. But after I had given this answer two or three times it became apparent to me that it was not the right one. The skyscrapers, I found, on pursuing the matter further, were ideologically incorrect. They had been Stalin's idea and now, since de-Stalinization, were regarded as being too closely linked with the cult of personality to be entirely respectable. I can only hope, for the sake of all concerned, that their fall from favour will not be permanent. Half a dozen or a dozen full-sized skyscrapers are not an easy thing to laugh off.

The whole question of Soviet art and architecture is a fascinating one. For some reason, one expects in this country of the Revolution to find the abstract art and rigidly functional architecture of a Brave New World. Instead one finds, in art, socialist realism, which in practice is indistinguishable from the bourgeois realism of the late nineteenth and early twentieth centuries, from Millais's 'Bubbles' and John Collier's 'Sentence of Death', and in architecture and decoration an unashamed return to the most exuberant classicism. Sometimes, as in the case of the skyscrapers, enthusiasm has got the better of good taste and the result bears little relation to anything. But sometimes the architect of this or that public building has stuck so closely to his classical model that, although reasonably expert in such matters, I found it hard to say whether I was looking at a new building or at one that had been built a hundred and fifty years ago. Amazing, too, is the stupendous lavishness of what one sees, of the marble and the gold and the bronze and the porphyry and the alabaster.

One evening I was taken by some friends to dine at the Praga, now generally regarded as the smartest restaurant in Moscow. My pre-war Baedeker informed me that it had enjoyed a similar reputation before the Revolution, and having a liking for Edwardian and Victorian survivals I was delighted by the glittering uniform and long forked beard of the obsequious old commissionaire on duty at the door, and even more so by the marble and gilt and plush and sparkling chandeliers of the actual restaurant which, as a monument to the eighteen-nineties, rivals Maxim's itself.

The dinner was worthy of the surroundings: caviar served in a block of ice, cutlets à la Kiev, that masterpiece of culinary art that somehow imprisons hot melted butter inside a fried wing of chicken, and Glace Plombière, an ice made of real cream. (The Russians, though progressive in other respects, have not yet got around to making ice-cream from soya beans, melted down horse-hooves, and the waste products of coal-tar.)

'It is easy to see,' I said enthusiastically to my companions, 'that nothing here has been touched for the last fifty years.' 'On the contrary,' they replied, 'the whole place is absolutely new. The old Praga, which was nothing like so grand, was flattened by a bomb during the War.'

For the past twenty years I had had a faint feeling of guilt, for the reason that during the whole of my previous stay in the Soviet Union I had somehow managed to avoid a visit to the Moscow Underground. 'Yes,' an aged Kirghiz nomad in the wilds of Central Asia had once said to me pityingly, after I had admitted to him that I had never actually been on the Moscow Metro, 'I can understand that for a man who had never before seen such a thing it would indeed be frightening.' But this time there was no escaping it. 'Tomorrow morning at nine o'clock,' said the pretty little *sputnitsa*, or female sputnik, allotted to me as a tourist de luxe, 'we will visit the Metro.'

I must admit that, although I had been prepared for it, the Metro took my breath away. It was like something out of Revelation. Each station was different and each more heavily and fantastically adorned than the last, with bronze and gilt, with statues and bas reliefs, with porphyry and alabaster and malachite. The average Soviet citizen may live in utter squalor at home, but at least when he travels by Underground he can enjoy unparalleled splendour.

By Metro we travelled, with one or two changes, to the Agricultural Exhibition. Once again I gaped. Having passed through a tremendous triumphal arch we found ourselves standing at one end of a vista facing an even more tremendous pillared pavilion, topped by an immense gold spire and bearing a strong family resemblance to the Admiralty at Leningrad. The sun was shining. A pleasant breeze chased white fleecy clouds across blue sky. Flags were flying. From loud-speakers poured forth ceaselessly a stimulating selection of jazz, marching songs and Viennese waltzes. Immediately in front of us was an enormous fountain lavishly adorned with colossal symbolic female figures of glittering gold. On either side of the central avenue were the pavilions of the various republics of the Union, each designed, as near as possible, in the national style of the republic concerned, some European, some oriental, all highly dramatic. Over each pavilion flew its own national flag. Inside were piles of produce, instructive tableaux, statistical charts and other devices designed to inform the visitor about the economic and agricultural life of the republic concerned. All were filled with crowds of visitors listening openmouthed to enthusiastic commentaries delivered by native representatives of the territories concerned. It was all

34

rather agreeable and immensely imperial, a kind of super-Wembley. Few Russians, I reflected, could have gone away without feeling proud to be citizens of so great an empire. Which was no doubt what was intended.

Another Moscow sight that I now saw for the first time was the inside of the Kremlin. Though I had lived opposite the Kremlin for two years I had never in fact been into it, for the simple reason that in Stalin's day it was kept firmly and ineluctably shut — a holy of holies from which the profane were excluded. But now you had only to get yourself a ticket, and with a crowd of several hundred other people, Russians and tourists alike, you could wander for as long as you liked round the palaces, the cathedrals and the museums. You could, if you liked, go and gaze from close-by at the building outside which are drawn up the shiny black motor cars of the men who rule the Soviet Union. You could, if you liked, even take out a camera and photograph it.

This in itself was significant. And so, in a different way, was the barbaric splendour of it all: of the cathedrals and churches with their gilded onion domes, their ikons, their frescoes and their massive gold screens, and of the imperial treasures in the museum. Here was the ivory throne of Ivan the Terrible; the jewelled bridle of Catherine the Great; a horse-blanket entirely made from orange parrot feathers; a crown containing 3800 large diamonds; a scale model of the Trans-Siberian Express in platinum and gold. To me it seemed to provide, in a way, the historical background for much else that I had seen:

for the gilt and marble and bronze of the Metro stations, for the magnificence of the Agricultural Exhibition and the architectural extravagances of the skyscrapers. Glitter and colour mean a lot to the Russians. In old Russian the word for 'red' and for 'beautiful' was the same. Which is why for centuries before the Revolution the Red Square bore the same name as it does now.

The same side of the Russians' character which leads them to seek refuge from the drab bleakness of everyday life in bright colours and, on occasion in the vodka bottle, also draws them irresistibly to the drama in all its forms: to the theatre, the opera and, above all, the ballet. For these they have a natural gift and a natural appreciation. As chance would have it the Moscow State Ballet, to which for the past twenty years I had been promising myself a return visit, was away in Paris. And so there was no ballet at the famous Bolshoi Theatre. But, on making inquiries, I found that *Swan Lake* was being given that evening at the smaller Stanislavski Theatre and that there was still a chance of getting a ticket.

The Stanislavski Theatre has a tradition and a charm all of its own. With its plain classical white-columned galleries and boxes and dark red velvet curtain it is less overpowering and more intimate than the more magnificent Bolshoi. It would, I thought, be interesting to see what they made of *Swan Lake*. And so, after hastily swallowing as much caviar and vodka as I could get through in ten minutes (food and drink, I find, greatly heighten my appreciation of any dramatic performance), I slipped into my seat a minute or two before the curtain went up.

Nothing is more nostalgic, nothing more evocative than certain pieces of music, except, perhaps, certain kinds of food and drink. In a flash Chaikovski's overture, coming on top of a substantial quantity of caviar and vodka, carried me back twenty years to my lost youth, to my early days as a diplomat and budding balletomane. Settling in my seat I waited happily for the curtain to go up on the familiar, old-fashioned and faintly ridiculous scenery and costumes which I had seen so often before. But when it did I found that I was witnessing a different and, to my taste, better presentation of *Swan Lake* than what I had been accustomed to see at the Bolshoi. Not that it was in any way revolutionary (perish the thought!). On the contrary, it was all pure socialist realism. But it was socialist realism at its good, old-fashioned, nineteenth-century best.

Being a conservative (with a small as well as a large C), I have a sneaking weakness for socialist realism. Though, I hope, enlightened and even progressive in other respects, I enjoy being able to see for myself without undue difficulty what a work of art is intended to represent. On this score, the Stanislavski company's presentation of *Swan Lake* did not cause me a moment's anxiety. It told the story and it told it with immense, with superb gusto. The forest glade was intensely romantic. The lake, whether sparkling in the sunlight or glittering in the moonlight, was exactly like a real lake. The wicked magician, hovering hideously with huge, sinister, shabby wings that somehow suggested both a bat and a bird of prey, was utterly horrible. The court ball was twice as magnificent, twice as regal as any real court ball has ever

37

been. Finally, the climax when it came was superbly dramatic. The magician, flapping his great black wings in a frenzy of malevolence, caused a violent storm to agitate the surface of the lake. Amid thunder and lightning great waves swept across the stage. But in the end good prevailed over evil. The magician was drowned in his own highly realistic waves, the storm subsided. And Odette and her Prince, she in a small golden crown and a delicious pink nightdress, emerged serene and triumphant in the rays of the setting sun. It had been an immensely enjoyable evening.

Technically, perhaps, the dancing of the corps de ballet fell short of the supremely high standard of the Bolshoi. But any shortcomings on their part were more than redeemed by the superlative dancing of Vinogradova, the prima ballerina. Still at the outset of her career, she had in addition to virtuosity the slender gracefulness of youth. She danced, too, with an intensity of feeling which I have never seen rivalled: in the role of Odette, with tenderness and grace; in the role of Odile with a hard glittering brilliance that matched the black sparkle of the jet spangles on her dress. How agreeable for once, I thought, to witness the early triumphs of a ballerina who has risen so quickly and who has clearly such a great career before her, rather than the perhaps more finished but less spontaneous performance of a seasoned star of long standing.

The rest of the audience evidently thought so too. As the old familiar story, swept along by Chaikovski's music, gradually unfolded itself, and in each scene Vinogradova, warming to the applause, danced better than in the last,

38

they became more and more excited, more and more enthusiastic. At the rise of the curtain the seat next to me had been empty. But half-way through the first act I looked round in the dark to see sitting in it a thin, pale, shabbily dressed little boy of about fourteen, who had clearly somehow slipped in without a ticket. And now he was sitting spellbound watching every entrechat and pirouette, and applauding with the knowledge and appreciation of an expert. Looking about at all those rapt faces, I found it hard to believe that these frenzied enthusiasts were the same stolid, respectable, rather pompous men and women who in the interval paraded decorously up and down, bowing and smiling to their friends and staring approvingly at each other's glittering uniforms or smart satin dresses.

What it comes to is that nobody enjoys a spectacle more than the Russians. They enter into the spirit of it, lose themselves in it, become part of it. It was the same a day or two later at the football match between Great Britain and the Soviet Union. It was admittedly a frantically exciting match, ending in a draw: 1-1. But the immense crowd which packed every inch of the vast stadium was like no football crowd I have ever seen. It was not that they were especially noisy. It was just that they were beside themselves with excitement.

And how, I asked myself, about the Orthodox Church which for so many centuries supplied almost alone so many of the innate needs of the Russian people: their need for a faith, their deep-seated need for orthodoxy as such, their need for a hierarchy, their hunger for colour, for music, for a spectacle, a legend, for something to take them out of themselves, to lift them above the drabness and squalor of everyday life?

A visit to Zagorsk, or Sergievo as it was formerly called, an ancient place of pilgrimage some sixty or seventy miles from Moscow and now once again the seat of an important Orthodox seminary, gave me a chance to examine one or two aspects of this question.

Topping a slight hill, as you approach Zagorsk from Moscow, you suddenly find yourself confronted with the watch-towers and massive pink and white outer walls of the famous fortified monastery of St Sergius, from inside which rise in splendid profusion the fantastic spires and domes of half a dozen churches. Of these the largest and most striking is the sixteenth-century Cathedral of the Assumption with its five bright blue onion domes lavishly sprinkled with shining golden stars. Here in a plain unornamented tomb is buried Boris Godunov. Near the cathedral stands an elegant five-tiered pink and white baroque campanile built in the middle of the eighteenth century by the Italian architect Rastrelli. Inside the precincts heavily bearded monks and theological students go about their business singly or in pairs, while throngs of pilgrims and sightseers wander from shrine to shrine and the bells ring out wildly from all five tiers of Rastrelli's bell-tower.

I had not been at Zagorsk for long when I received a message to say that the rector would be glad to receive me and hoped that I would stay to luncheon. On being ushered into his presence (the cliché describes the process exactly) I found him to be a dignified old gentleman in black robes with a fine white beard and a large pectoral cross. On the wall behind him was an enormous portrait of Lenin.* There were also a number of ikons and holy pictures. Lenin, I noticed, had pride of place. But despite the manifest discrepancy between Lenin, who had called religion the opium of the people, and the holy ikons which looked down from their golden frames, I formed the impression that the rector was not necessarily an insincere man. During the last forty years he had, no doubt, on occasion had to compromise. But he would not have been the first religious leader to do that. And, compromise or no compromise, his path over the last forty years could not, I judged, have been an easy one.

How, I asked him, did he account for the change which there had been during the last twenty years in the attitude of the Soviet Government towards the Orthodox Church? When I had last been in Russia the Church was being savagely persecuted. Now I understood that this was no longer so.

The answer, he replied, was quite simple. During the War, the Soviet Government had made the discovery that the Orthodox Church was a perfectly patriotic body; that it was possible for a man or woman to be a believer and yet a good Russian patriot. And so their attitude towards it had changed. It was now recognized that the Church had a place in society. Seminaries were allowed for training young priests. The members of the hierarchy

---

* As a distinguished American visitor to Zagorsk recently observed: 'The rector's predecessors in office would have turned in their graves at this. But then so would Lenin.'

were invited to official functions. Only yesterday the
Patriarch Alexei had been officially received by Mr
Khrushchov. During the War some of the church leaders
had actually been decorated by the Soviet Government.
(He did not, however, say what I had also noticed —
namely that on occasion the dignitaries of the Orthodox
Church issued pronouncements on political, and particularly international matters which might have been dic-
tated by Mr Khrushchov himself.)

Where, I now asked the rector, did the Church get its
money from? Was it subsidized by the State? No, he
replied, the Church received no funds from the State.
It was entirely supported by voluntary contributions from
the faithful, which were more than enough for its needs.
All the State did was to give authority for the release of
building materials where they were needed for repairing
churches, and for paper and printing facilities when these
were required for printing Bibles and so on. Over these
sort of matters, he added, and over taxation the authorities no longer discriminated against the Church, but were
for the most part reasonably helpful.

And what, I asked, had been the effect on the Church of
this respite from persecution. The effect, he replied, had
been good. There had been what amounted to a religious
revival. More churches were open. A number of disused
ones had been reconsecrated. There were more priests
and bigger congregations. The subscriptions to church
funds were necessarily small, but there were lots of them.
The women, as always, were a great stand-by. But whole
families now came to church, and the children told other
children about it and brought them too. The number of

believers was growing all the time. More and more couples were getting married in church. The churches remained open all day and more and more people went into them to pray quietly by themselves. This, he believed, was a sign of true religion. In this way, he concluded, a new Christian society was coming into being. 'We have,' he said, 'a lot to thank God for.'

After the rector had said grace we sat down to luncheon. Being Tuesday, it was a fast-day. But there was wine and two sorts of caviar and smoked sturgeon and several other kinds of fish, which were pressed on us with great solicitude by the motherly female who waited at table. We were joined at luncheon by the rector's lay secretary, a nice old man who told me that he had served as an artillery officer in the Imperial Russian Army in World War I, a subject on which he reminisced at some length. He was now using his administrative talents to help the rector run the seminary.

When we had finished, I went across to one of the ancient churches that stood within the precincts. In the darkness of the church almost the only light came from the candles and sanctuary lamps, which in turn was dimly reflected from the gold of the screens and crucifixes and ikons. The first thing that struck me was the extreme beauty of the singing. Then, as my eyes became accustomed to the darkness, I gradually made out the faces of the congregation — old people for the most part, grey-bearded peasants in smocks and wrinkled old women with handkerchiefs round their heads, but with some young people and children amongst them, and all wearing the same rapt devout expression. Next to me stood a young

43

couple with a child, well dressed and prosperous-looking—perfect examples, one would have thought, of up and coming Soviet citizens — they, too, like the rest of the congregation, completely absorbed in their devotions. Outside, hearing more singing, I wandered into a small chapel where another service was in progress. This was dedicated to St Sergius, who founded the monastery in 1340. In front of the altar a spring of clear water bubbled up from a spout in the shape of a cross. The congregation clustered round it as they sang. 'Drink', they said to me. 'It is miraculous. It will purify you.' I scooped some up in my hands and drank it. It was ice-cold and had an odd metallic taste.

I had been struck by what the rector had told me and by what I had seen, and on my return to Moscow I made one or two further inquiries. Why, I asked, did the powers that be allow this religious revival, if such it was? Because, I was told, they no longer feared the power of religion and believed that, left to itself, it would in due course die out. Meanwhile, by tolerating it they gained the support of those sections of the population who were still religious. The Party line naturally still laid down that all religion was nonsense, and it was still impossible for a Party member to belong to any religious denomination.

This interested me. So did some figures which I saw quoted in the *New York Times* and which I have every reason to believe are reliable. According to these, in 1917 there were 46,000 churches in Russia and 50,000 priests. By 1935 there were only 4000 churches and 5000 priests. But by 1956 there were 20,000 churches and 35,000 priests. Meanwhile the Soviet Press has of late been commenting anxiously on the ever-increasing numbers of church weddings and baptisms and calling upon the civil authorities to brighten up their wedding ceremonies with music and confetti in order to be better able to hold their own.

I can't say that at the end of it I was left with any very clear impression of how things were really developing or were likely to develop in the future. It struck me as the sort of situation which people are apt to interpret in whatever way suits them best. But once again there had clearly been a big change since 1938.

Beyond Zagorsk the road leads on to Pereslavl and Rostov Jaroslavski and Jaroslavl, towns dating back to the dawn of Russian history and abounding in magnificent churches and monasteries, but not as yet included in any Intourist itinerary. Which made Patrick and Rachel Reilly's invitation to spend a weekend exploring them all the more attractive.

Our first stop was at Pereslavl, where by the side of a little river there was another fortified monastery like that at Zagorsk, containing a number of churches and one tiny, absolutely plain white cathedral with a single dark green onion dome, built in the year 1152 by Prince Yuri Dolgoruki, the founder of Moscow. Prince Yuri, I found, kept cropping up everywhere, and I was reminded of the splendid equestrian statue in the heroic manner recently erected to his memory by the Moscow municipal authorities.

After Pereslavl the road took us through a typical Russian landscape of birch and pine forests and wide flat fields stretching away into the distance. Every now and then the monotony was relieved by an untidy village of wooden huts or another fortified monastery. Then suddenly we came to an enormous expanse of water, with, far away beyond it, a line of pinnacles and domes glittering in the afternoon sunshine and reflected back again from the shining water. This, we decided, must be Rostov Jaroslavski and the lake, Lake Nero.

Continuing along the shore of the lake we arrived before the walls of a fine monastery, and were about to enter it by the main gate when a soldier waving a sub-machine gun ran up and drove us away. It was, he said, military and there was no admittance, while simultaneously an irritating little boy of seven or eight took up the cry 'Military! military!' Seeing that argument would be fruitless we decided to examine this particular ancient monument from the outside. But, trailing disconsolately along under the shadow of the massive crenellated wall, we almost at once came to a place where the latter had fallen down and there was an immense gap. And so, stepping through this, we made a leisurely tour of the churches and buildings within, while the soldier presumably continued on guard at the front gate. What, we wondered, could the military installation be that he was guarding? A petrol dump, perhaps, or a potato-store. But as far as we could see there were no signs of anything even vaguely warlike.

On coming out we found a jolly-looking woman cleaning some large lake-fish and throwing the insides to some cats which she had whistled up for the purpose. Always on the look-out for human interest pictures, I raised my camera. But at this her jolly face took on a look of horror and she leaped hurriedly to her feet, dropping the fish and scattering the cats. 'Why,' I asked, 'don't you want to be photographed?' 'Because,' came the reply, 'I don't want to have my picture taken doing something so uncultured as cleaning fish. And then you would take it back to your own country and say that Soviet people were not cultured.' I did my best to explain that in Great Britain people also clean fish. But it was no good and I had to go away without a picture.

A little farther on we came to the centre of the town and to another, larger, walled monastery. Here a *kapitalni remont* or complete overhaul was in progress, and a gang of robust-looking women labourers were carrying buckets up and down a ladder and balancing precariously on the roof-tops. These, I soon found, had no inhibitions about being photographed, but laughed their heads off at the idea and willingly posed for their portraits while perched in the most precarious positions. One in particular couldn't have enough of it. 'Again! Again!' she shouted, as my camera whirred and clicked. The churches which they were repairing were topped with fantastic gold and silver domes. It was these we had seen glittering in the sun across the lake. A covered passageway ran round the top of the battlements, linking the look-out towers one with the other. These were clearly serious fortifications. The museum and churches, we found, were shut, and so we decided to drive on to Jaroslavl and come back to Rostov on our way home next day. As we were starting, I saw in a shop window a complete outboard engine for sale and a variety of fishing tackle.

We reached Jaroslavl just as it was beginning to get dark. As Patrick's car — a Jaguar — drew up outside the hotel, an immense crowd immediately collected to look at it. By the time we had got out and taken our luggage from the boot we were surrounded. The crowd, by now wildly excited, stretched half-way across the square and soon policemen were arriving to control it. What make? What country? What year? What price? How many cylinders? How many kilometres an hour? shouted the onlookers, while we did our best to answer their questions.

Provincial hotels in the Soviet Union are apt to be rather a toss-up. This one, we were glad to find, had just had a *kapitalny remont* and everything was spick and span — the rooms bright and airy, the furniture newly upholstered, the beds spotlessly clean. Its name was *Myedvyed* — The Bear. (*Myed* is the Russian for 'honey' and literally *myedvyed* means 'honey-eater'.) Across the square stood a charming little theatre, built about 1750 in the purest classical style and still in use today.

In the hotel restaurant an orchestra was playing which could be heard all over the hotel. On coming down to dinner we were offered a choice of goose, turkey or sucking-pig. Scarcely had we sat down than a large hearty-looking man at the next table, seeing that we were foreigners, immediately engaged us in conversation and was soon telling us his life history. He had all his meals here, he said. By trade he was a *slesar*, a locksmith. Marshal Tito, I remembered, was also at one time a *slesar*. Is locksmith, I wonder, really the right translation? And what does a locksmith do, anyway, besides making locks and possibly picking them?

Jaroslavl is on the Volga, and after dinner we decided to walk down and look at it. It was pleasantly warm and the streets were full of people out for a stroll under the trees. The Volga we found to be an impressive stream, half a mile across, with the lights reflected in it and steamers chugging up and down. As we were standing looking at it, we were accosted by two of the usual friendly Soviet citizens, longing to talk to foreigners. These particular ones had had a good deal to drink and were inclined to sing. Then, finding that I understood Russian, one of them at once embarked on a long rambling account of how horrible life was in the Soviet Union. 'There is,' he kept saying, 'nothing to buy in the shops. Nothing, nothing, nothing!' 'Is it better than it was?' I asked. 'Yes,' he replied angrily, 'it used to be even worse.' In the middle of our conversation a militiaman walked by. At this my new found friend nudged me and pointed dramatically at the militiaman. 'And that —— there,' he shouted at the top of his voice, 'would arrest me for even talking to you.' Whereupon the militiaman, looking rather embarrassed, crossed to the other side of the street and walked hurriedly away. On our way back to bed we passed through a majestic eighteenth-century square in the middle of which stood rather a fine church, the Church of Elijah the Prophet.

Next morning we went to a densely crowded outdoor market where the peasants from the collective farms were selling their produce and where I managed to buy a particularly nice painted wooden toy popgun. After which, ignoring a State-sponsored poster which proclaimed in letters a foot high that tobacco is poison, I bought from the State-owned kiosk which stood immediately underneath it a packet of rather good State-produced cigarettes.

While I was making these purchases a woman came up and spoke to me in excellent English. I replied in English and she was delighted. 'It works! It works!' she said. She then told me that she taught English at a school, but had never before had a chance to try it out on anyone except Russians. Having complimented her on her accent, I told her that she must come to Great Britain. To this she replied that it had already been arranged that the headmaster of the school at which she worked should go and that she hoped that one day she might also. It was interesting to hear, even at second hand, of ordinary Russians being allowed to travel abroad.

On our way back to Moscow we again stopped at Rostov Jaroslavski to look at the churches and the museum. There we found the *remont* women again at work. This time they were sitting under a tree, making new metal crosses to go on the tops of the church domes. 'Vuot nash prijatelj!' they cried merrily as they saw me arriving with my camera. 'Here is our friend!'

The museum turned out, on inspection, to be very like any other provincial museum anywhere, only more so. It contained some early framed Bolshevik proclamations of the time of the Revolution; a stuffed hen sitting on an immense pile of imitation eggs and somehow illustrating the benefits of collectivization; and an early nineteenth-century portrait of an unknown lady, pale, willowy and mysterious, with masses of dark heavy hair. In the churches were frescoes of widely varying periods and of equally diverse artistic value.

Not far from Rostov we passed a funeral. The coffin, on a cart, was open and we could see the dead man's face like a waxen image, calm and dignified among the artificial flowers.

Our last stop was at one of the wayside monasteries we had passed the day before. It stood on a little hill surrounded as usual by massive fortifications. Peasants' houses clustered all round it as though for protection, and a long straggling avenue of silver birches led up to the gate. Inside there were two or three abandoned churches, fast crumbling into decay, and a handsome old house, once no doubt the residence of the abbot. In the afternoon sunshine some little boys practised throwing knives, while a couple of baby goats scuffled and butted each other in the dust.

On first arriving in Moscow in 1937 one of the first things I had done was to visit Lenin's red basalt mausoleum in the Red Square. Now, twenty-one years after, I went back there, slipping into the queue immediately behind a well-regimented East German youth delegation wearing cornflower-blue shirts (shirts again, I thought) and carrying with them a gigantic wreath. I wanted to see Lenin, lying in his glass case with his finely drawn features and his neat little beard pointed upwards. But even more, I wanted to see Stalin — Stalin whom I had last seen not in the mausoleum but standing on top of it, taking the salute at a ceremonial parade. And sure enough, when I had passed the motionless sentries at the entrance and been ushered down the black marble stairs into the brightly lit subterranean vault, there he was in his twin glass case, a squat grim figure, with his grizzled drooping moustache decorating his dead face, dressed in his special generalissimo's uniform with row upon row of medal ribbons on his chest, immensely formidable and immensely sinister. 'Move on, move on,' said the guards and, as we looked, we were herded along past the bodies and on up the stairs into the air and light.

By now I had been in Russia long enough to realize that Stalin's move from the outside of the mausoleum to the inside, from the perpendicular to the horizontal, from this world to the next, was by far the most important single change that had occurred in the Soviet Union since I had last been there. The War, of course, had left its mark — a grievous one — on the country and the people. It had also, by its outcome, revolutionized Russia's position in the world. But the basic internal changes that I saw all round me undoubtedly sprang in the main from the disappearance from the active scene of the grim squat little man in the glass case.

Almost the first thing I had noticed as I walked about Moscow was that the people in the street no longer wore the same terror-stricken look as before. There was no longer the same atmosphere of constraint. The passers-by now looked relatively cheerful and chattered unconcernedly about all manner of things. Amongst the young, in particular, there was as much laughter and joking and desultory flirting as anywhere else. Only occasionally, in the face of an older man or woman, did one see all too clearly reflected what they had been through in the past twenty or thirty or forty years.

Undoubtedly there had been an all-round relaxation of tension, a virtual cessation of the reign of terror that existed in Stalin's day. The secret police were still there, but they were much less in evidence and their powers had been greatly reduced. Foreigners, it is true, were still spied on and in embassies hidden microphones were still regularly found concealed behind tapestries and picture-frames. But the methods employed were less obtrusive and the waste of administrative effort involved, one imagines, less appalling. Before the War I had been constantly trailed by as many as four men. This time nobody, as far as I could make out, ever bothered to follow me, or go through my papers or touch my films or inspect my luggage — a sign of neglect on the part of the competent authorities which, I felt, verged on the insulting.

Not that Russia had in any sense become a free country. People were still arrested and there were still concentration camps for political prisoners. But their population was now much smaller and most of the inmates were there on more or less clearly defined charges, and not as the result of vague denunciations brought against them by almost anyone.

There had, too, been a marked falling off in the number of actual executions — witness, in particular, the number of Khrushchov's own rivals or opponents, Malenkov, Kaganovich, Molotov, Zhukov, Bulganin and the rest, who, though publicly disgraced for 'anti-Party activities', at the time of writing still remain not only alive but apparently even members of the Party.

As a result of all these changes there was, I very soon found, no longer the same paralysing atmosphere of morbid fear and suspicion; nor the same reluctance to accept responsibility; nor the same utter terror of being seen talking to a foreigner which I had found everywhere twenty years before.

Another thing that struck me immediately was how much better dressed the people were, both men and women. They also looked healthier and better fed. Their complexions were clearer and the girls were more skilfully made up. Twenty years ago a foreigner in Moscow had stood out a mile. Now, this was no longer so. By the standards of Bond Street or the Rue de la Paix the Russians were drably, drearily and shoddily dressed. But there were now many of them who could have mingled unnoticed with the crowd in the less prosperous streets of Manchester, Milan or Marseilles, and you often had to look twice at a passer-by to tell whether he or she was a foreign visitor or a Soviet citizen. Indeed, the wife of one diplomat living in Moscow told me that her little boy of seven, who was in the habit of playing in the street dressed 'as he considered that a tough little Canadian should be dressed', had come running in one day with a handful of small change which a benevolent old Russian lady had pressed into his hand, thinking that such a shabby-looking child could only be a beggar. And it is a fact that Soviet children, in Moscow at any rate, are as smart as paint: the boys, for the most part, in grey tunics and peaked uniform caps, the girls in neat black dresses with white collars and red bows on their pigtails, looking for all the world like illustrations to a nineteenth-century children's book.

Again, as I had seen for myself on the way in from the airport and elsewhere, enormous blocks of new working-class flats were now being built in enormous numbers. Not by Western standards very large or very luxurious flats, and still not in large enough numbers to meet the urgent needs of the rapidly increasing population. But at least the buildings were now going up, and families still living under appalling conditions had some hope that some day they would really be allotted the minimum dwelling-space to which they were nominally entitled.

There were also far more cars on the streets than before the War. Then, practically the only cars to be seen in Moscow were official cars and those belonging to foreign diplomats, with the result that the streets were almost empty. In those days it was almost inconceivable that a Soviet citizen should own a car. Now the Soviet output of cars has increased considerably and it is by no means unheard of for someone in the higher income groups to have a car of his own. There are not more than three or four different types to choose from, their prices are high and there are long waiting-lists for all of them, but people do buy them and may actually be seen taking their friends and relations for joy-rides in them. Thus motoring is now no longer confined to high State and Party officials and the volume of traffic, though still slight by Western standards, is very much heavier than it was. This increase in traffic has incidentally been followed by the introduction of a series of new and immensely complicated traffic regulations which are enthusiastically enforced by large numbers of militiamen on point duty. To find a petrol pump, however, is still difficult, and during my stay I personally only saw one in the whole of Moscow. Meanwhile, the population — especially the younger section of it — are becoming more and more car-minded, and any foreign car that draws up at the side of the pavement is at once surrounded by an excited crowd of enthusiasts, many of whom display surprising technical and mechanical knowledge.

A great many foreigners arriving in Russia for the first time would be far from impressed by all this, for the reason that they would be judging what they saw by the standards to which they themselves were accustomed. And what they saw would compare anything but favourably with what they were used to in London or Rome, in Paris or New York, in Stockholm or Copenhagen. On the contrary, they would in all probability be shocked by what would no doubt strike them as an atmosphere of repression and constraint, by the incessant propaganda, by the lack of amenities, by the shortage of what they would regard as the necessities of life. But my judgment (and the judgment, incidentally, of most adult Soviet citizens) was based on the almost inconceivably low *Soviet* standard of before the War. And, by pre-war standards it could not be denied that there was an all-round improvement.

There was, for example, an obvious improvement in the quality and quantity of the consumer goods offered for sale in the shops. Walking through GUM, the great arcaded State department store, across the Red Square from the Kremlin — visited daily, it is said, by more than 130,000 customers — I was amazed at the change. Here were fashionable hats, fancy shoes, strapless evening dresses, smart city suits, an abundance of complicated cameras, watches and jewellery, radio and television sets, elaborate children's toys, a great variety of expensive scents, a rich choice of food, wines, spirits, cigarettes and tobacco. The necessities of life might not always be readily obtainable. But in GUM, at any rate, there seemed to be no lack of luxuries. There were far more goods for sale than before the War. There was a far wider choice. And the quality was far better. But this was not to say that in any of these respects they compared with the goods for sale in the shops of any Western European country. Or that most people could necessarily afford to buy them.

This brings us to the question of price. And here the inquiring foreigner immediately comes up against the tricky problem of how to calculate the true value of the rouble. He will, for example, find in one of the windows of GUM a man's ready-made brown lounge suit of inferior quality. He will observe that it is priced at 1500 roubles. He will work out that this, at the official rate of exchange of eleven roubles to the pound, is about £134, or more than a dozen times what a much better suit would cost in London. Surely, he will think, something must be wrong. He will next try calculating on the basis of the average wage. This is round about 750 roubles a month, or rather more than twice the guaranteed minimum wage of 350 roubles. He will then find that to buy such a suit will cost the average (as opposed to the lower-paid) industrial worker the whole of his wages for two months — which means that he will not be able to replenish his wardrobe very often. He will also find, if he bothers to go at all closely into the budget of anyone trying to live on the minimum wage of 350 roubles, that the margin between him and starvation is very narrow indeed. On the other hand a leading scientist or technician, a factory director or university professor, earning, as is quite usual, 15,000 roubles or £1340 a month in addition to numerous perquisites and privileges (and probably paying not more than about 12 per cent of his income to the State in tax) can clearly afford to be better fed and better dressed. From which our investigator, though still without a very clear idea of the true value of the rouble, will correctly conclude that there is such a thing in the Soviet Union as rationing by price and that a wide disparity exists between rich and poor, between privileged, under-privileged and unprivileged.

Neither phenomenon is by any means new. Both existed twenty years ago. But in present circumstances they have both acquired a new significance. The saying, current in Moscow, that the strength of Khrushchov's position lies in the fact that he is moving away from socialism as fast as we in the West are moving towards it is perhaps a little unfair to all concerned. But there is certainly much in the Soviet Government's lavish use of incentives and differentiation, in their deliberate building up of a privileged class, in their chauvinism and their tendency to take more account of human nature, that would shock our own old-time Butskellists.

'Under Stalin,' said Khrushchov in a recent off-the-record conversation, 'the whole machine was rapidly becoming paralysed.' In other words, the Generalissimo was treating his subjects so mean that they were ceasing to be keen. The terror was defeating its own object. After thirty years of blood, sweat and tears the Industrial Revolution was now an accomplished fact. Like everything else that had ever happened to them, it had been imposed on the Russian people from above, brutally, by main force. It had been achieved virtually by the massive use of slave-labour. (The magnitude of Stalin's personal achievement has yet to be generally recognized.) Now, as in our own industrial revolution, a phase had been reached where different methods were called for, where to produce the desired results more attention must be paid to the human element, to the standard of living of the workers — to the production, in a word, of consumer goods, where inducements must somehow be found to persuade the peasants to play their all too important part in the programme.

Khrushchov's answer has been to slack off quite considerably on the stick and substitute a fair amount of carrot. Not nearly enough carrot to go round, but enough to give some Soviet citizens their fill and others a good chance of getting a nibble if they exert themselves sufficiently; enough, in other words, to enlarge substantially the class which has a vested interest in the continuance of the regime.

To enlarge it. And also to give it continuity, to make of it a regular ruling class, which in Stalin's day, owing to the high casualty rate among the top people, to the rapid turnover caused by shooting, it never really had a chance of becoming. There are, it appears, people in the Soviet Union who earn, in one way or another, as much as a million roubles a year. This at the official rate is £90,000, or at a more realistic rate, say, £20,000. But even regarding this as exceptional (which it is), there are certainly relatively large numbers of Soviet citizens who earn the equivalent of several thousand pounds sterling a year. Now, in the Soviet Union the highest rate of income tax is 13 per cent. These fortunate people therefore keep by far the greater part of what they earn. They can also invest it in Government securities which give a reasonable return. If they like they can spend part of it on building or buying themselves a house. They can buy themselves one or more motor cars. And finally, when they die, they can leave their possessions and what money they have saved to their children, the highest rate of death duties being only 10 per cent. Thus, in addition to enjoying numerous advantages of upbringing, an upper-class child in Russia may with reasonable luck also expect to inherit from his father a considerable sum of money and will thus inevitably have a very different start in life from the son of a low-grade worker on a State farm in Eastern Siberia.

This brings us to perhaps the most important development of all: the emergence over the years of a new aristocracy, in the main an administrative and technological aristocracy, better educated and harder to bully or bamboozle than the general run of Soviet citizens, far more demanding in every respect and absolutely essential to the maintenance of Russia's existing rate of economic, political, military, technical and scientific progress.

It is impossible to spend any length of time in the Soviet Union without becoming aware of the existence of this new class which exists alongside and to some extent independently of the Party. It is they who have the big salaries, they and their families who drive or are driven in the big cars, occupy the new flats, build themselves country cottages, wear expensive clothes, eat in smart hotels, shop in luxury shops. They have a thirst for what they call 'culture' ('Down with culture,' cried Dostoyevski, 'the thirst for culture is an aristocratic thirst'). They have the confidence, the self-assurance of a firmly established ruling class.

And so have their children, who by merit, by influence or just by knowing the ropes find their way to the universities and technical colleges and military and naval academies; who, with their girls, occupy the best seats in the theatres and cinemas; and who in restaurants and night-clubs attract attention by their fashionable style of dress, uninhibited behaviour and easy mastery of the latest developments in American jazz. 'Olga Ivanovna! Olga Ivanovna!' said the loud-speaker on a Black Sea pleasure steamer as it came into harbour. And, as a pretty smartly dressed teen-ager appeared from a luxury-class stateroom (for there are four classes on these steamers): 'This is to inform Olga Ivanovna that her maid and her motor car are awaiting her at the dockside.'

'Under God and the Tsar', ran the old saying, 'all men are equal.' In Imperial Russia there was no old-established aristocracy, no bourgeoisie, nothing in short that you could call a proper ruling class. The same was even truer under Stalin. But now, forty years on, under Stalin's successors, a ruling class is fast emerging — a class of capable, ambitious men and women who are ready, indeed determined, to play their proper part in affairs and to have their proper share of the rewards. Such in England, one imagines, must have been the behaviour of the new up-start aristocracy under the Tudors, and again two or three hundred years later of the suddenly enriched scions of the Industrial Revolution.

With Victorian England in particular there are many parallels to be drawn. There is the same rapid industriali-zation with all its attendant sacrifices, human and other-wise, the same sudden economic expansion, the same emergence of a new, confident, self-assertive class, the same earnestness, the same will to power, the same belief in progress, the same sense of their country's imperial destiny, the same agreeable, absolute certainty that they are right. It is even possible to carry the parallel further. Like their Victorian counterparts the new Soviet aristo-cracy are priggish, prudish, inclined to be pompous, rigidly attached to their own vested interests and rigidly conservative in their ideas and in their profound reverence for the Establishment in all its manifestations. Even their tastes are the same: they like pictures and statues that are easily comprehensible. They like rich solid food and rich solid ornate decorations and furnishings.

But, the reader will say, are not these worthy people all Communists? Do they not all believe in world revolution? Of course they do. They are Communists just as the Victorians were Christians. They attend Communist Party meetings and lectures on Marxism-Leninism at regular intervals in exactly the same way as the Victorians attended church on Sunday. They believe in world revolution just as implicitly as the Victorians believed in the Second Coming. And they apply the principles of

Marxism in their private lives to just about the same extent as the Victorians applied the principles of the Sermon on the Mount in theirs. Neither more nor less.

How cynical! the reader will say. And of course, humanity being what it is, few things are more conducive of cynicism than to observe stage by stage the evolution of any revolutionary movement. Once your revolution has taken place, a flaming revolutionary faith is something which it may well be neither possible nor desirable to keep alight. 'Une révolution', says André Malraux, who is an expert in these matters, 'ne maintient sa victoire que par une technique opposée aux moyens qui la lui ont donnée. Et parfois même aux sentiments.'

Happening to take shelter from a sudden thunderstorm I found myself one day in the Lenin Museum. Room after room was filled with relics of the dead leader — copies of his pamphlets, picture postcards which he had sent from exile in Switzerland or Italy, reports of his speeches, illicit revolutionary newspapers, photographs of him in Siberia, fancy oil paintings of the more dramatic moments of the Revolution. As I watched, organized groups of bored Soviet school-children followed their guides from room to room, while their guides, prim middle-aged women with pince-nez, explained to their charges, in the high expressionless sing-song peculiar to guides, who Lenin was and what he stood for. It was like the ancient Egyptian department of the British Museum or a not very exciting Sunday school. Only once did I detect a momentary flicker of interest: from two little boys who had broken away from the rest of the party and were carrying out a private investigation of the ancient

Rolls Royce in which Lenin had once driven round the streets of Moscow.

For all that it would be a mistake to underestimate the strength of Soviet communism. It is quite true that the members of the Soviet Communist Party and of the new ruling class that is now arising in the Soviet Union are, in the true sense of the word, revolutionaries neither by training nor by temperament. For them, as one penetrating commentator has put it, 'Leninism has been transformed from an ideological dynamic into the source of the new respectability.'* They are pillars of society who believe in their country right or wrong. One can quite easily see them, in other circumstances, queuing to join the Carlton Club, becoming brigadiers or bishops or company directors or magistrates or masters of hounds. One can in no circumstances see them in the role of rebels against established authority, of long-haired rabble-rousers or Angry Young Men, addressing protest-meetings in Bloomsbury or making clever, querulous contributions to the columns of *Tribune* and the *New Statesman*. But the society of which they are pillars is a Communist society and their country is the Country of the Revolution. For them Communism and all that it stands for may not be a flaming revolutionary faith, but it is a state of mind, a mental attitude, a deep conviction which it would take a very great deal to shake or undermine. It is the sheet anchor, the common belief, the orthodoxy, so necessary in one sense to the Russian temperament; while what they call 'Capitalism', however vague their conception of it may be, is the enemy, the anti-Christ, something the

* Edward Crankshaw, *Russia Without Stalin.*

64

Pereslavl: the Cathedral

GUM: Shopwindow

Moscow University

The Cathedral of St. Basil,
Red Square

mere mention of which automatically shocks their deepest susceptibilities.

And yet ... ideas are strong things. Human nature will in the long run assert itself. And there is much about Communism that is contrary to human nature. Given the chance, no one is more human or more susceptible to new ideas than the Russian, especially the young Russian of today. Stalin, who knew this, though he was not a Russian, believed for his part in taking no chances, in granting no freedom, in admitting no outside influences, in allowing no discussion, in shooting first and investigating afterwards. And who is to say that from his point of view he was not right? 'You are blind,' he said to the assembled members of the Politburo not long before his death, 'like little kittens. What will happen without me?' It is a question which has still to be answered.

Until you actually get to the Soviet Union it is almost impossible to imagine the fantastic importance which is attached there to education, especially technological and scientific education, not only by the Soviet Government but by every Soviet citizen one ever meets. This enthusiasm for education already existed twenty years ago. Since then the efforts of all concerned have redoubled. Every town of any size has its university or technological institute. What is more, these efforts have been more than justified by results. Illiteracy has to all intents and purposes been abolished and the Soviet Government now not only have at their disposal a comparatively large number of top-level nuclear and other scientists but, equally important, are fast building up a vast pool of lower- and medium-level scientists and technicians, which twenty years ago was completely lacking.

I have seen the figure for Soviet citizens possessing advanced education put as high as six million. And, of course, quite clearly a modern technical society cannot be made to work by mere hewers of wood and drawers of water. But here again there is another side to the picture. People who have been trained to think and to think to some purpose about engineering, nuclear physics and higher mathematics, will probably sooner or later start thinking about other things as well. And if there are enough of them so engaged the result is going to be extremely interesting.

Particularly fascinating to me were the social and political implications of what I saw in the course of a couple of hours' visit to Moscow University. In view of the emphasis placed by the Russians on scientific and technical education it is perhaps appropriate that the scientific section of the University should be housed in the highest and most spectacular new building in the Soviet Union. Situated in a commanding position on the Lenin Hills, it is built in the exuberantly classical super-Palladian style which the Russians, after various less happy experiments, seem finally to have adopted as the standard pattern for their public buildings. A soaring central tower, higher than many American skyscrapers, is flanked by two massive wings. Within, there is the same abundance of pillars and pediments as without, together with the usual profusion of porphyry and alabaster, of gilt and bronze. The statistics, as one would expect, are formidable: 17,000 students, 15,000 rooms, 1900 laboratories, 113 lifts, 66 miles of corridors.

But what interested me most were the students themselves. For here, it occurred to me, was the cradle of the new aristocracy. In the first place there was, as far as I could see, nothing distinctively Soviet about them. To me they looked very much like students at any other university anywhere else. And this struck me as being in itself significant. Both boys and girls wore the same sloppy, fanciful clothes by which in most countries academic youth shows its contempt for convention. They showed, too, as they paired off in twos and fours the same healthy interest in the opposite sex as youth, whether academic or not, does anywhere if left to itself. And as they came pouring out of the lecture rooms there was the same shouting and laughter as one would hear in a Western university. In short, they did not in the least give the impression of 17,000 well-drilled, well-disciplined automatons.

Nor, indeed, are they. It is no secret that in Russia, as elsewhere, the university students are more unorthodox, not to say more subversive, in their views than any other class of the population. It is here amongst the academic youth that the hunger for new ideas, for information about the outside world which is characteristic of the population as a whole, reaches its climax, its boiling point. Here less and less is blindly accepted, less and less taken for granted; already the first doubts, the first questionings, the first signs of cynicism, are beginning to appear. Small wonder that anxiety on this score is from time to time reflected in the utterances of the Party leaders.

Small wonder, too, I thought, as I shot up and down in the 113 lifts and padded along the sixty-six miles of corridors, looking in, as I went, on reading-rooms and lecture rooms and theatres and laboratories and observatories and marble swimming-pools and lavishly equipped gymnasia in which shapely young women in bathing-dresses were carrying out intricate physical exercises on parallel bars — small wonder that a new class with a new outlook is rapidly coming into being. In the ordinary way a student spends five years at the university, probably the most formative years of his life. During these five years he lives, by Soviet standards, fantastically well. He is paid a salary of from 300 to 500 roubles (at par £27 to £45) a month, supplemented, if he works well, by substantial bonuses. He receives, according to various distinguished foreign educationalists who have had the opportunity of judging, an extremely sound education. He is, in all probability, exempted from military service. In most cases he has a small, bright, comfortably furnished room to himself, sharing a bathroom between two. He can eat on the premises in a number of well-equipped special cafeterias which offer a wide selection of dishes at extremely low prices. He has at his disposal, without ever leaving the precincts, a variety of magnificent swimming-pools, playing-fields, gymnasia, cinemas and, surprising though it may seem, an enormous and remarkably well-stocked university library of Russian and foreign books. He is also encouraged to organize excursions, dances, dramatic performances and various kinds of sporting events and is given the most lavish assistance for the purpose by the university authorities. Finally, having once

68

graduated, he is assured, providing he behaves himself, of an interesting and well-paid job and of a privileged place in society for the rest of his life.

When you compare the lavish, carefree existence of these fortunate young people with the hard life of the average Soviet citizen, sleeping as often as not six in one squalid room, queuing endlessly for the bare necessities of life, queuing for every kind of pass and permit, struggling through rain and mud and snow to get to his work, struggling to get away from it, burdened with domestic worries, fighting for his few pleasures, you can understand the fierce competition there is to get into a university and the determined efforts made by the more influential members of Soviet society to see that their own children and those of their friends and relations are among the successful candidates. You can understand, too, the sense of their own intellectual and social superiority and importance which all but the most exceptionally modest graduates of such an establishment must feel on completing their five years at it.

Against this background how far, I asked myself, would it be possible for Khrushchov to put the clock back? Could he, if he wished, revert to a reign of terror on Stalinist lines?

The answer, it seemed to me, was that an attempt to reintroduce Stalinist methods, even if it succeeded, would in all probability cause such dislocation as not to be practical politics. Nor does it in fact seem likely that Khrushchov has any wish to revert to Stalinism. He is a tough, clever, flexible man who is prepared to take risks and who should on no account be underestimated. He no doubt reckons that by his present methods he can produce better results. And he is almost certainly right. He may even succeed, as he has said he will, in catching up some day with the American standard of living and of production.

And yet he is on a slippery slope. The more freedom he gives people the more they will want, especially the new aristocracy. The more he improves their standard of living the greater will be their demands. The more influence he allows the new aristocrats the more unassailable their position will become. In short, if any one thing about the Soviet Union seems probable it is that in ten years from now the character of the Soviet regime will be appreciably different from what it is today.

Apart from everything else there is the question of contact with the outside world. How far can such a system safely be exposed to outside influences? How far can its discipline be relaxed, without in the long run basically altering its character?

The present rulers of the Soviet Union do not seem unduly worried by this possibility. Rightly or wrongly they no longer appear particularly nervous of the contaminating effects of foreign contacts. Indeed, they seem to feel that in their long-term struggle for world power they have something to gain from them. After years of isolation, after years of tirades against 'cosmopolitan' influences, they have finally accepted the idea that they might have something to learn from the West.

And so, to an ever greater extent, they are encouraging

foreigners to visit the Soviet Union and are even allowing a few, a very few, Soviet citizens to go abroad. A corner, if a very small corner, of the Iron Curtain has been lifted. Today in the Soviet Union it is no longer really dangerous for Soviet citizens to meet and talk to foreigners, and such is the natural friendliness of the Russian people and their hunger for information about the outside world that, if he chooses, a Russian-speaking tourist can spend as much time as he likes in interminable conversations with Russians of every sort and description. This in itself is an immensely important change. 'Are things better here now?' I asked a man of about my own age who had sat down at my table in a restaurant. 'Yes,' he replied, 'very much better. Otherwise you can be quite certain that I should not be sitting talking to you like this.'

These were the preliminary impressions which I formed during my first week in Moscow, and it was against this background that at the end of that week I set out in a spirit of excited anticipation on the next stage of my journey.

TWO

TURKESTAN DE LUXE

A WEEK or two before my departure from England it had been announced in the Press that the Russians had closed Central Asia to foreigners. They were, so it was said, testing bombs or launching rockets in the waste spaces of Turkmenistan, and no one could go there until they had finished. At the Soviet Embassy the officials concerned had been amiable but inclined to evade the point. Could I, I inquired, cross the Caspian by boat from Baku to Krasnovodsk? The Capsian Sea, they replied non-committally, was full of submarine oil-wells which made navigation very difficult. Better wait till I got to Moscow and arrange the details of my itinerary there.

And so, after what had seemed such a promising start, I had arrived in Moscow still not absolutely certain in my own mind whether I should really get to Central Asia or not, even as a tourist de luxe. My first interview with the Intourist official responsible for British tourists quickly dispelled all my doubts. I could fly to Tashkent whenever I liked, he said, and what was more by jet aeroplane. And to Samarkand? To Samarkand too. Only Bokhara was difficult. But that, also, could probably be arranged on the spot.

My doubts did not revive until a day or two before the date fixed for my departure from Moscow, when I was suddenly told that I could not go after all. The whole of Central Asia, it seemed, was full of literary men. From all over the world, delegations of littérateurs were flocking to Tashkent. They had booked all the seats on all the aeroplanes and filled all the rooms in all the hotels. There was no room for me anywhere. 'But I, too,' I said, 'am a literary man.' 'No,' they replied firmly, 'a tourist de luxe. Quite a different category.' Perhaps, they suggested, to pass the time, I would like to give an interview to Radio Moscow on my travel plans. The suggestion, I replied, struck me as ill-timed.

There followed a day or two of uncertainty. Could it be, I wondered, that they were not going to let me go after all? Then, after one or two false alarms, I was told that seats had been reserved for my *sputnitsa* and myself on the aircraft leaving for Tashkent next day. And sure enough by an early hour next morning we had driven out to the airport, and having found the right queue were waiting our turn to emplane in company with a number of distinctly Central-Asian-looking characters, one of whom, mysteriously, was carrying in his arms a large fresh pineapple. We were off at last.

The giant TU-104 jet air liner, with its sixty comfortable armchairs, brown and gold wallpaper, lace curtains, china figurines in glass cases and heavy mahogany tables, covered the 3000 kilometres from Moscow to Tashkent in three and a half hours. From a height of 20,000 feet one was vaguely aware of the fields and forests of European Russia, of the Volga, of the Sea of Aral, and later, as we ate our neatly served breakfast of fresh caviar and *escalopes de veau*, of the arid expanse of the Kizil Kum.

Then came the warning to fasten our seat belts, the rapid circling descent and, suddenly visible through the tilted window, the green avenues and gardens, the orchards and tree-lined watercourses of Tashkent. Remote above the haze to the south-east rose a barrier of snow-capped mountains. As the doors were opened and we stepped out into the glaring sunlight of Central Asia, the heat hit us like a blast from a furnace.

A palatial suite — bedroom, drawing-room and bathroom—had, I was glad to find, been reserved for me at the principal hotel, which according to a marble plaque let into the wall had served as Bolshevik headquarters in Tashkent during the Revolutionary War. In the entrance hall photographs of distinguished visitors to Tashkent were prominently displayed, amongst them one of my former colleague in the House, Mr Tom Driberg, beaming happily from the middle of a cluster of young Uzbeks. In the ornate plush-curtained restaurant a frenzied orchestra was playing selections from *Carmen*, while a powerful soprano in a royal blue off-the-shoulder evening dress soared courageously above the hum of conversation, the rattle of plates and cutlery, and the buzz of the electric fans. It was very hot. In one of the windows a deliciously pretty Chinese girl sat with her father, drinking Uzbek champagne. But most of the customers were locals — a mixture of Russians and Uzbeks, of bureaucrats, technocrats and manual workers, some blue-eyed and fair-haired, others dusky-hued with high cheekbones and almond eyes, some come straight from work in their shirt-sleeves and shovelling down their food voraciously, others elegant and sophisticated. The food, when you got it, was rather

74

good, part Eastern and part European. The vodka and the beer were ice-cold. Feeling refreshed and invigorated by my late luncheon I set out in the sweltering afternoon heat to explore the town.

Ever since it was first laid out in the 'seventies and 'eighties of the last century as capital of the recently conquered province of Turkestan, and seat of the Russian Governor General and Commander-in-Chief, the new town of Tashkent with its broad poplar-lined avenues of solidly built bungalows, reminiscent in a way of the cantonments of a garrison town in British India, has remained separate from the old mud-built native quarter on the other side of the valley, with its mosques and minarets, its flat-roofed houses and its labyrinth of narrow winding streets. But this distinction will not survive much longer. Today, with a mixed population of over a million inhabitants, Tashkent is capital of the Soviet Socialist Republic of Uzbekistan and, in theory at any rate, there is no distinction between Uzbeks and Russians. What is left of the old town is rapidly disappearing. Part has already been replaced by new avenues and blocks of flats and by an immense sports stadium, and more is now being demolished to make way for a vast new hotel designed, I was told, to house the visiting foreign *sportsmeni*, or athletes, who will perform there, and for a gigantic Park of Rest and Culture.

Disappearing, too, are the national dress and national customs of the inhabitants. Only a few old men wear the turban. Only a very few women wear the *paranja*, the traditional thick black horsehair veil which completely covers the face. Even the *khalat*, the brightly striped many-coloured robe of Central Asia is rarely to be seen. Only the *tibiteika* survives universally, the little embroidered skullcap originally designed to serve as base for a turban. In Uzbekistan, as in the other more exotic republics of the Union, the standardization and Sovietization of everything is proceeding apace, especially in the towns.

The Mohammedan way of life, once so deeply rooted in Russian Central Asia, dies hard. Twenty or thirty years ago the Soviet authorities were still having trouble with the mullahs. But now there are no signs of a conflict. To-day, Islam is no longer a menace or even a nuisance to the Soviet Government. Indeed there are even signs that it might from their point of view have positive advantages and become, paradoxically, a not unimportant instrument of cold war policy in the Near and Middle East.

While I was in Tashkent the Grand Mufti of Central Asia, Ziyouddin Khan Ibn Mufti Khan Babakhan, on hearing that I wished to see him, was kind enough to ask me to dinner with him in the sixteenth-century *medresseh*, or religious college, which adjoins his mosque. The meal, which began with the traditional breaking of flat unleavened Uzbek bread, was served in a high airy whitewashed room adorned with bright green tiles bearing a text from the Koran. Some doves which nested in a brass chandelier flew in and out through the open trellis-work as we ate. Round the heavily laden table sat the imams of the other mosques in Tashkent, half a dozen dignified elderly gentlemen with long white beards, dressed in plain grey or white robes with large white turbans.

The Mufti himself was an astute-looking man of about fifty with a thin black beard, wearing the traditional white turban and a brilliantly coloured robe of bright yellow, green and red stripes. Our conversation followed almost exactly the same lines as those which I had had with the rector of Zagorsk and other dignitaries of the Orthodox Church in European Russia. His relations with the Soviet authorities, said the Mufti, left nothing to be desired. He did not receive financial help from them; for that he depended on voluntary contributions from the Moslem population. But they showed themselves generally co-operative, provided facilities for the restoration and maintenace of mosques, and last year had enabled him to print an edition of the Koran for the first time since the Revolution. The number of practising Mohammedans was now on the increase, more mosques were open, and a limited number of young men were being trained up as mullahs, some here in Tashkent and others in Bokhara.

Did he, I asked, have any contacts with Mohammedans in other countries? Yes, he said, he did. Of late there had been a great many Moslem visitors from abroad. Only a week or two before President Nasser himself had worshipped in one of his mosques, and there had been other visitors from many other Mohammedan countries.

After taking my leave of the Mufti I went off to a gala performance in the portentous new opera house, given in honour of the President of Finland who had just arrived in Tashkent. The costumes and scenery of the opera, which was sung in Uzbek and dealt with some episode in early Uzbek history, were lavish beyond words — all scimitars and cloth-of-gold and pleasure-domes and beautiful slave girls in transparent trousers. It was immensely long, and though enjoyable was about as Eastern in spirit as *Chu*

77

Chin Chow or *Madame Butterfly*. Between the acts the President of Finland, a neat Nordic-looking man in a sensible blue suit, was taken to a room leading out of the foyer and given refreshments by the local notabilities. Next week, they told me, they were expecting the King of Nepal.

The King of Nepal, I thought, as I climbed wearily into bed, the President of Finland, President Nasser, Moslems who came to see the Mufti, sportsmen who performed in the stadium, Chinese girls drinking champagne, distinguished political visitors who stayed in the hotel: Tashkent was fast becoming the hub of Asia, a veritable epicentre of attraction for swanning notabilities. But, for my part, I could not wait to get to Samarkand and Bokhara which had been the high spots of my pre-war journeys of twenty years ago.

'Samarkand,' said the Head of the Intourist office in Tashkent, 'you can go to. Samarkand is on our itinerary. But not Bokhara. Bokhara is not allowed. If you wanted to go to Bokhara, you should have said so in Moscow.'

'But I did say so in Moscow. And in Moscow they told me that you would be able to arrange it here.'

'No. Not here. In Moscow.'

'In that case, ring up Moscow and ask for permission.'

'It will do no good.'

'Do it all the same.'

'All right. I will do it while you are in Samarkand.'

But I had a pretty good idea what the result would be.

*

An hour and a half after taking off from Tashkent the expertly piloted if rather ancient twin-engined aircraft taxied to a standstill, and collecting my luggage I scrambled out into the brilliant sunshine. The air was cooler and more exhilarating than it had been in Tashkent. Facing me was a flimsy wooden arch, bearing the inscription SAMARKAND. On one side of it stood a large silver-painted statue of Lenin; on the other an equally large silver-painted statue of Stalin. In front of these were two beds of Michaelmas daisies. Through the arch a car was waiting for me with Pyotr Petrovich, a robust-looking European Russian, in the driving-seat. I climbed in.

For five or ten minutes we drove across the dusty, barren expanse of the Afrosiab. On either side of the road a wilderness of crumbling ruins and ancient graveyards stretched away into the distance. This was once the site of the city of Maracanda, founded, it was said, by Alexander the Great. Then suddenly we topped a rise and came all at once in sight of the minarets and glittering turquoise domes of Samarkand, spread out before us against a background of brilliantly green gardens and trees. Away on the horizon above the blue heat haze rose a range of distant snow-capped mountains.

From where we were I could distinguish the three great *medressehs*, or religious colleges, which form the three sides of the Registan, or principal square. Near by rose the vast shattered arch of the mosque of Bibi Khanum, the Chinese princess who became Tamerlane's wife. To the south stood the Gur Emir, the blue-domed tomb of Tamerlane himself; and just outside the city to the north

79

the clustered cupolas of the Hazreti Shakh Zindeh, or
Shrine of the Living King, an avenue of ancient tombs and
shrines dating back to long before Tamerlane, built on
either side of a flight of steps up the side of a hill. Soon we
had reached the Old Town and I noticed that since
my last visit a neat little public garden, with another
silver-painted statue of Stalin in his greatcoat and
peaked cap, had made its appearance next to the
Registan.

From the dust and hubbub and crowds of the Old
Town we passed rapidly to the broad, leafy avenues of the
New. 'There,' said Pyotr Petrovich, pointing proudly to a
massive new building in the approved classico-oriental
style, 'is the Philological Faculty of the University of
Uzbekistan. And there is the stadium. And here, until
the new one is finished, is the hotel.'

The hotel at Samarkand bore a family resemblance to
the hotel at Tashkent. In both the furniture consisted
of mass-produced bedroom suites of light polished wood.
The plush portières were identical — evidently a general
issue to all provincial Soviet hotels. The pictures, too,
were the same. In the course of my travels I was to become
quite attached to a coloured lithograph of 'Three Baby
Bears at Play in a Forest Glade', which, in various sizes,
adorned practically every hotel I stayed in. In Tashkent it
had been in my sitting-room. Here, it was in the entrance
hall.

In addition to the picture of the three baby bears the
entrance hall, which was painted chocolate colour and
was full of people, also boasted a large gilt chandelier and
a heavy wooden frame, four feet high by two feet wide,

The Grand Mufti and his Imams.

'And now would I
photograph their children

Chaikhana

containing a list of nineteen rules to be observed by hotel guests. The hall porter, a mahogany-skinned Uzbek with high cheekbones and a pair of long jet-black drooping moustaches which gave him an almost Chinese air, sat by the door, deep in conversation with a friend. He wore a bright blue uniform with a broad triple band of shining gold braid running round his peaked hat, round his collar and cuffs and down the outsides of his trousers. The reception desk had a seething crowd of people on both sides. On it was a telephone, down which from time to time one or other of them shouted. Over by the entrance door was another telephone. A man in a panama hat was talking down it, assisted by two more men in panama hats who were advising him what to say. Several more people were standing near by, listening and waiting for their turn to telephone. Somewhere in the background a man was practising on the trombone.

Inside the hall it was dark and cool. Through the street door one could see the brilliant green of the trees and the dazzling glare of the midday sun. On one side of the door was a glass-topped case containing a few rather disappointing picture postcards of polar bears sitting on ice-floes. Behind it sat a pale, detached-looking girl in a black dress. In another glass case were three electric razors, five bottles of Soviet scent, a cake of soap and a selection of embroidered skullcaps. Through another door was a barber's shop with one man being shaved and several others waiting their turn. Yet another door had a curtain across it. Pulling it aside I found, as I knew I eventually should, three shapeless, sensible, middle-aged women with handkerchiefs tied round their heads and pudgy Russian faces sitting patiently in a row. Having entrusted myself to the care of one of these I was taken to my room.

After I had duly booked in and dumped my luggage I set out to rediscover Samarkand, plunging at once into the variegated crowd that thronged the bazaar. In the Old Town of Samarkand, to a far greater extent than in Tashkent, the inhabitants have retained their national dress and way of life. In the bazaar, in the tea-houses or *chai-khanas*, on Fridays in the mosques you may still see any number of men wearing turbans and brightly coloured *khalats*, while here and there in the street you will occasionally catch sight of a completely veiled woman.

I was also able, I found, to talk to far more people and see far more than I had expected of local life. I had only to walk through the streets with my cine-camera to be at once engaged in conversation by literally scores of passers-by: old and young, men and women, Russians and Uzbeks. Where, they wanted to know, did I come from? And where had I learnt Russian? And what did I think of the Soviet Union? And how much did my trousers cost? And why had I come to Samarkand? And why did I walk when I could travel by tram? And would I photograph them? And now would I photograph their children and their brothers and sisters and their old, old grandfather? I had only to sit down in a *chai-khana* or a public park to become the centre of an animated group, some asking me questions and others telling me things. Only in the outdoor bazaar where the peasants from the country round

82

market their wares (no longer, under the new law, at fixed prices, but for what they will fetch) was the vast seething crowd so excited by the business of buying and selling that they would hardly have looked up from their bargaining if the Prophet himself had strolled by.

It is not true to say that Samarkand has been spoiled. It has just been tidied up, and in the process it has lost a little of its charm. Previously when I visited the Gur Emir, the tomb of Tamerlane, with its magnificent turquoise-blue dome, I was let in after a good deal of grumbling by an old man in a turban whom I found sleeping in the dust under a mulberry tree in the fore-court. Now the forecourt has been neatly cemented and I was shown round the jasper-lined burial chamber by a certificated guide. But it is only fair to say that the structure, which would otherwise soon have collapsed, has now been expertly shored up and restored so as to be good for another three or four hundred years.

Cement or no cement, the Gur Emir remains to my taste the most beautiful and the most enthralling building in Samarkand. Nothing else can quite equal the serene majesty of its great blue ribbed dome. And, if one has any sense of history at all, it would be hard not to be moved as one stands looking down at the plain narrow tomb-stone of dark green jade from Chinese Turkestan which marks the tomb of Timur the Lame.

Restorations are also being carried out on the mosques and minarets of the Registan, of which Lord Curzon, who visited it in 1888, wrote that it was 'the noblest public square in the world'. Here, round the vast cobbled square, the restorers have set up their workshops in the

cloisters and cells of the adjoining *medressehs*, where, with
infinite care and employing the identical methods that
were used in the time of Tamerlane, they have at last
managed to produce glazed tiles of exactly the same
consistency and shade of blue as those which they are
replacing.

Though I would not myself go as far as Lord Curzon,
no one I think could fail to be impressed by the splendour
of the three great *medressehs* of the Registan: Tilla Kari,
the Mosque of Gold; Shir Dar, the Lion-Bearer; and
Ulug Beg, the oldest of the three, built in 1434 by Tamerlane's grandson, the astronomer of that name, whose
observatory can still be seen on one of the hills outside the
town. Even the travelling concert-party, or *ansambl*, of
telegraph girls from Tashkent, in whose company I
inspected them, momentarily ceased their cheerful chatter
as we walked through the grass-grown courts and stood
looking up at the soaring arches, the slender minarets, the
splendidly rounded domes and the great yellow lion that
sprawls across the front of the Shir Dar.

But a sense of pride in the historical monuments of
their town is something that is not shared by all the citizens of Samarkand. 'Look at him,' said a high local official
of the Society of Cultural Relations with Foreign Countries, pointing angrily at me as I clambered about the
superb tombs and shrines of the Shakh Zindeh with my
camera. 'He has been round all those old ruins *twice*. I
know why. He is *photographing* them, and then he will go
home and say that the whole Soviet Union is full of
nothing but ruins.'

But, for my part, I went on photographing in colour

'A completely
veiled woman'

'Buying and selling'

The Gur Emir.

and in black and white, in still and in motion pictures. At the head of the narrow stairway stands the tomb of the Living King himself, Kassim Ibn Abbas — a royal martyr who, it is said, lurks to this day at the bottom of a neighbouring cistern, with his head beneath his arm, still alive and ready when the time comes to emerge and claim his kingdom. Lower down the hill, on either side of the walled passage-way, are the blue-domed tombs of Tamerlane's old nurse and of his two sisters. And at the foot is the entrance arch built by his grandson Ulug. For centuries the Shakh Zindeh has been a place of pilgrimage, and though today it is officially classed as an ancient monument, and not as a place of worship, during the whole of the time I was there there was an intermittent stream of surreptitious worshippers who slipped unobtrusively into one or other of the holy shrines to prostrate themselves and pray.

After my conversation with the Mufti of Central Asia I was anxious to see for myself how the mosques were attended. A couple of days after my arrival at Samarkand it happened to be a Friday, and so at about midday I made my way to the principal mosque of the city. As I approached it I saw that a great concourse of worshippers, for the most part older men in turbans and brightly coloured *khalats*, were already assembling and spreading their prayer mats, row upon row, in the open space beneath the balcony in which the imam had taken up his position. Soon they were overflowing into the public garden outside. Then, as the high wailing cry of the muezzin sounded from the minaret, the assembled multitude prostrated themselves as one man and worship began, the vast congregation repeatedly bowing down and standing up again and intoning the responses and prayers. In the haggard bearded faces around me I saw the same look, the same dedication, the same intensity of feeling as I had seen in the Christian churches in European Russia — the look of those who attend divine worship because of some inner compulsion, overriding all worldly considerations, and not just because it happens to be the right thing to do.

But already my *sputnitsa* was waiting to take me off to see a collective farm. Like the man from the Society for Cultural Relations, she seemed to regard the pleasure I took in ancient monuments as slightly morbid. Nor did she much care for my interest in Moslem religious observances. A collective farm, however, was by any standards ideologically correct and her pretty little face wore an expression of quiet satisfaction as we bowled along the white dusty road and out into the country.

After driving for half an hour or so between flat cultivated fields we passed under a rather flimsy wooden triumphal arch, and drew up in front of a plain squarish building which turned out to be a kind of community centre. In front of this stood a portly and inscrutable-looking Uzbek, waiting to welcome me: the President of the collective farm.

Having shaken hands, the President took me indoors into a room containing a conference table and a gallery of pictures, including a large one of himself, wearing a medal and looking as portly and inscrutable as ever. Would I, he

inquired, like to ask any questions? I responded with the
sort of questions that one always asks when being taken
round other people's farms. How many acres? How many
men? How many head of sheep and cattle? What breeds?
How were they doing? What sort of harvest last year? What
sort of harvest this year? After which we set out on a rapid
tour of his domains: vineyards, orchards, potato fields,
pasture, arable, horses, cattle, sheep, then suddenly an
underground network of deep covered trenches in which
were growing lemon trees.

By now it was late afternoon, and, as I had eaten nothing since seven that morning, my thoughts were beginning
to turn more and more persistently to the subject of food,
when all at once we came to a graceful rustic pavilion
idyllically situated at the side of a tree-shaded pool and
looking like an illustration to Omar Khayyám. Here a
carpet had been spread and preparations seemed to be in
train for a meal, or at any rate for refreshments.

Thankfully following the President's example I sat
myself down cross-legged beside him on the carpet. Here
we were joined by a talkative middle-aged lady who kept
noisily repeating that she was the mother of seven
children, and by a character who was introduced as the
Brigadier. The Brigadier was mahogany-coloured and had
the finest pair of drooping black moustaches I have ever
seen in Central Asia or anywhere else. His appearance at
first sight was doleful, but he turned out on acquaintance
to be the most friendly of men. The brigade which he
commanded was an agricultural shock-brigade and he
was immensely proud of its achievements. On discover-
ing that I, too, had once been a brigadier of sorts, he

was overjoyed at the coincidence. A bottle of vodka was produced and we drank to the health of brigadiers of all kinds and all nations; then to farming; then to mothers of seven; and then to anything that came into our heads. The vodka was followed by some dry bread, which was ceremonially broken, a plate of pistachio nuts and some green tea. Being very hungry and thirsty and not quite certain how much more was coming, I ate and drank everything I could get. But there now followed in rapid succession a large number of flasks of excellent local white wine, some soup, a great hash of mutton and a veritable mountain of pilaf or *plov* — rice cooked in mutton fat — followed by more green tea and more vodka and by a selection of strange-looking sweetmeats. Squatting or reclining, with fingers that got greasier and greasier, we ate and ate and ate. 'Try using a fork,' said the Mother of Seven officiously from time to time. But it was no good.

'Have some snuff,' said the Brigadier wiping his fingers and passing me a small brown highly polished gourd from which he shook a little pile of bright green snuff. '*Not* up your nose,' he added as I took a pinch. 'Under your tongue.' By the time he had taught me the Central Asian way of taking snuff and I had taught him the European method there was snuff pretty well everywhere. 'Keep it,' he said delightedly. 'Keep it all.' And before me as I write lies the Brigadier's little polished snuff-gourd full of green snuff from Samarkand. Its stopper ends in a special little horsehair whisk to whisk away any surplus grains of snuff. It is a useful little contraption and recalls a memorable meal.

By the time we had eaten, drunk and snuffed our fill,

the poplars were casting long shadows over the vineyards and the sun was sinking below the western hills. It was time to go home. As we piled into the car the Mother of Seven thrust into my arms an enormous bouquet of full-blown pink roses. Then Pyotr Petrovich let in the clutch with a jerk and, while the governing body of the collective farm stood waving us goodbye, we shot off through the triumphal arch in the direction of Samarkand, entirely enveloped in a cloud of fine white dust.

That night when we got back to the hotel, I felt somehow like going to a cinema. There was an outdoor one, they told me, in the Park of Rest and Culture. Strolling down the street from the hotel past the Officers' Club (still, I noticed from my 1914 Baedeker, occupying the same site as in tsarist days), I bought a ticket and sat waiting under the brilliant starlight of Central Asia for the film to begin. Round me, boys and girls held hands and cuddled exactly as they do in democratic countries; necking was no longer 'uncultured' or ideologically incorrect.

The film, when it began, was also a sign of the times — a comedy about two men, one tall and one short, and a blonde, also a comic television announcer, a retired Red Army general with a big white moustache, who was exactly like any other retired general of the screen or stage, and a number of other more or less relevant characters, all of whom ran, skidded, stumbled and fell through their breathtakingly knockabout roles and through a succession of skilfully contrived misunderstandings in the approved film-comedy manner.

It carried so far as I could make out no conceivable ideological message, nor indeed any other very clearly

defined message, unless it was that while, even in the
Soviet Union, the course of true love does not always
run smooth, boy is apt to get girl in the end. But it was a
welcome change from the smug little moral tales, each
with a carefully hammered home socio-political point,
which passed as light entertainment in the Soviet Union
in the late nineteen-thirties.

Next night there was a change of film, so I went again.
But though the title and the actors were different the film
was to all intents and purposes the same. Again there was
a blonde with two young men after her, this time pursuing
her in shiny streamlined sports cars to the exclusive
holiday resorts of the Black Sea Riviera. And again came
the same happy ending, while a contented audience held
hands and sucked sweets in the starlight.

Back at the hotel I came on a man and a girl who were
listening intently to the wireless: Forces Favourites,
relayed from Radio Ceylon. 'Our next number,' said the
reedy-voiced B.B.C. announcer, 'comes to you at the
special request of Mrs Higginbotham of Wigan, Lanca-
shire, for her son, Corporal Cyril Higginbotham, whose
birthday it is today: Elvis Presley singing "Dixieland
Rock".' But I, for my part, went thankfully off to bed. I
had had enough light entertainment and gathered enough
disparate impressions for one day.

As I continued to trudge through the thick white dust
from *medresseh* to mausoleum and from mausoleum to
medresseh, the Central Asian sun blazed down on Samarkand and the distant blue mountains that hung in the

haze between earth and sky far away on the horizon in the direction of Persia looked infinitely alluring. Could I, I asked, go there? Rather to my surprise I was told, after some hesitation, that I could. And sure enough next morning at the appointed hour the burly Pyotr Petrovich was waiting at the door of the hotel with his Pobyeda motor car, a packet of sandwiches and a bottle of vodka. We set off, and, after two hours' fast driving across the fertile cultivated plain that lies to the south of Samarkand, reached the foothills and started to climb. All along the road, which was not at all a bad one, we met little groups of countrymen in turbans and *khalats* starting out on their ponies and donkeys to ride into Samarkand.

Our destination was a former Mohammedan place of pilgrimage, a grove of ancient elms growing round a deep shady pool. From its clear depths bubbled up a spring of fresh water, the source of a rushing mountain stream which flowed out through a great stone ring set in the verge of the pool. Any young woman, they told us, who swam through it back and forth two or three times would have any number of children. Near by was a disused mosque and by the pool knelt an old man praying. 'He is weak in the head,' they said pityingly. 'He prays and prays all day.'

The elms, it seemed, were eight hundred years old. They had been there long before Genghiz Khan or Tamerlane. In the hollow space under the roots of the largest of them there was room for twenty men. In the troubles after the civil war during the 'twenties this area had been a hotbed of *Basmachis*, the nationalist rebels who had gone on fighting the Bolsheviks for ten years after the Revolution. Looking at the wild precipitous tangle of mountains above us I could see that it would have been good country for guerrilla war. But now it seemed the most peaceful place imaginable. To one of the immemorial elms someone, no doubt in order to make himself feel at home, had pinned a small coloured reproduction of the three baby bears.

As I was thinking how agreeable all this was after the glare and dust of the town and settling down to eat my sandwiches, we were hailed by three young men who on further inspection proved to be grilling kebabs on skewers over a charcoal fire. Would we not join them, they asked with spontaneous hospitality, and with an eye, I suspected, to the charms of my *sputnitsa*. They had a day off from their jobs in Samarkand and were spending it together out here. One was a local Uzbek, one was a Tadjik from Stalinabad and the third was a Tartar with a Jewish mother. There was plenty for everyone, and if we needed some more lamb or some more bread we could get it from the near-by village of Urgut.

Twenty minutes later we were sitting cross-legged with our hosts on a kind of flat platform by the side of the pool in the shade of one of the great trees, the vodka and some bottles of beer were cooling in the spring and we were eating the best kebab I have ever tasted, with homemade cream cheese, cherries, apricots, spring onions and flat round loaves of Samarkand bread, so famed for its excellence that in the old days the Emir of Bokhara would eat nothing else.

After luncheon I set out with one of our hosts, a teacher at a technical college in Samarkand, to climb in the hills

Shakh Zindeh

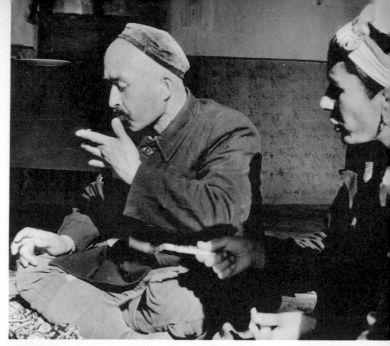

'Try using a fork'

Urgut

which rise abruptly above Urgut, while the others remained behind to sleep under the shadow of the trees. Eventually, after a long steep scramble, we reached a point from which we commanded a tremendous view of the plain as far as Samarkand and beyond. High above us rose the jagged mountains of Tadjikstan. 'Do you know Randolph Churchill?' asked my companion. I replied that I did.

On the way down we met a Tadjik girl from the near-by village, a slight, graceful figure as she stood watching the fat-tailed sheep that cropped the short sweet grass of the mountainside. She spoke fluent Russian and was filled with an unquenchable thirst for knowledge about the outside world. I asked her whether she minded being photographed and she replied that there was nothing she would like better. She was, she told us, engaged to be married. We asked her the name of the biggest mountain in the range above us, a grim formidable peak that rose steeply above the rest. 'The Mother-in-Law,' she said, and burst out laughing.

When, a little later, we rejoined the rest of the party at the spring, we found that they had stripped off their clothes and were splashing gaily about in the water, merrily pushing my prim little *sputnitsa* back and forth through the magic stone ring. Following their example we plunged in too. By the side of the water the old man was still praying oblivious to everything that was happening round him.

But already the shadows had begun to lengthen and we felt ready for some more kebab before setting out on the return journey to Samarkand. As we were packing up we were joined by the little Tadjik shepherdess, who had come down to be photographed again. 'Come back soon!' she said, waving her hand as we finally drove away. Back at the hotel the trombonist was still hard at work, practising his trills and quavers.

Next morning I flew back to Tashkent. There was some delay at Samarkand Airport, and while I was waiting to emplane I listened to the announcements that were being broadcast over the loud-speaker. 'The aeroplane for Bokhara is about to take off,' said the announcer, and as I watched a rather battered-looking little passenger aircraft trundled down the runway and took off in a westerly direction. Soon it was out of sight. In about half an hour, I reckoned, feeling thoroughly frustrated, it would be landing at Bokhara. The question was, how to get on to it? But my continually renewed representations to Intourist got me nowhere at all.

Twenty years ago my original approach to Soviet Central Asia had been by way of Kazakstan. After first travelling by train half-way across Siberia I had dropped off at Novosibirsk and then made my way unobtrusively south by the Turksib, the new railway line linking the Transiberian with Turkestan. This had brought me to Alma Ata, the capital of Kazakstan; and from Alma Ata, travelling westwards, I had eventually reached Samarkand. Some months later I had paid a further visit to Alma Ata, but on this second occasion I had been firmly but politely put on the train by the police and sent back to Moscow under an expulsion order. Despite this temporary

94

setback my memories of Alma Ata were happy ones and
I was now anxious, if possible, to go back there.

There would, said the representative of Intourist,
assuming with relief that I had finally given up the idea of
going to Bokhara, be no difficulty at all about my visiting
Alma Ata. I could fly there direct from Tashkent. Could
I go by train? I asked. No, he said. Plane, not train.
Trains were not suitable for tourists; not that train,
anyway.

It didn't seem worth arguing about. And so, no sooner
had we landed at Tashkent Airport on our return from
Samarkand, than I was hurried off across the tarmac to
where another twin-engined aircraft was waiting with
twirling propellers, ready to take off for Alma Ata.

From Tashkent our course lay north-east. On our
right rose a great snow-capped barrier of mountains; to
our left the plain stretched away endlessly to the north —
stretched away, I calculated, without so much as a hillock,
for 2000 miles to the Arctic Ocean.

The Soviet Socialist Republic of Kazakstan, for the
capital of which we were now bound and which I suspect
a great many people have never heard of, is larger than
the whole of Western Europe put together. Its area
extends over more than a million square miles. Its population, on the other hand, is small — only eight and a half
millions. And a great deal of its territory consists or consisted of desert. Under the tsars, it was a place of no great
importance. The Kazaks and Kirghiz who inhabited it
were wandering nomad horsemen who with their flocks
and herds ranged over vast areas of country, pitching their
circular skin tents where they could find pasture and

possessing no fixed abode. Alma Ata, or Vierny, as it was then called, was a remote garrison town which had been founded in 1854 and which by the turn of the century could still boast no more than 20,000 or 30,000 inhabitants. Most of these were Russians. Its good climate and fruitfulness made it suitable for colonization by Europeans, and the Imperial Government encouraged peasants, retired soldiers and other European Russians to settle there. In Kazak 'Alma Ata' means 'Father of Apples', a name which it thoroughly deserves, for the apples grown in the orchards which surround it are the finest both in size and flavour that I have ever tasted anywhere.

Alma Ata's real importance as a town dates back to the opening in 1931 of the Turksib Railway which linked it up with the rest of the Soviet Union. In seven years its population increased from 50,000 in 1931 to 230,000 in 1938. It has since increased by another 100,000 to 330,000. Of these about two-thirds are European Russians and the remainder native Kazaks or Kirghiz. These vary considerably in type. Most of them have flat round moonlike faces with high Mongoloid cheekbones and look rather like Esquimaux, but some have oval faces with acquiline features of a more Persian type. Nearly all have dark reddish-brown complexions like those of North American Indians. Some of the women still wear strange high medieval-looking headdresses; the men wear long padded coats and, on their heads, skullcaps, round fur hats or helmet-shaped cones of thick white felt with sharply upturned brims. But already European clothes, even among the native population, are almost universal. Kazak, like most of the tongues of Soviet Central Asia, is akin to Turkish; to the Kazaks Russian is a foreign language. Though most of the Kazaks are now no longer nomads and have exchanged their tents for villages of mud huts, they are still born horsemen naturally at home in the saddle.

Of recent years Kazakstan's economic importance has increased still further. It is a real boom country. It now produces more copper, lead and zinc than any other republic in the Union and is third in production of coal and oil. It is also the biggest producer of sheep and cattle, and its grain production is in the neighbourhood of sixteen million tons a year. This is partly the result of Khrushchov's Virgin Lands Project which, in a spectacular attempt to increase Soviet agricultural output, has brought something like 100 million more acres under cultivation in Kazakstan and south-west Siberia in the last five years. Whether or not this ambitious undertaking will succeed remains to be seen. Some observers are sceptical and talk gloomily of dust-bowls and ultimate catastrophe. But Khrushchov is by nature a gambler. The project is a bold one and if it does succeed will go some way towards solving the problem of Soviet agriculture, which is one of the most worrying ones that he has to face.

As our aircraft approached Alma Ata I could see, looking out, gigantic areas under cultivation, immense rectangles of green and brown where before there had been nothing but howling wilderness — The Virgin Lands. Then the flaps went down and a few minutes later we were skimming along the tarmac of the runway.

Alma Ata is magnificently situated. Immediately behind it — an immensely dramatic backdrop — rise the

G 97

snow-capped peaks of the Tien Shan, or Mountains of Heaven, the great mountain barrier which divides Russian Central Asia from Chinese Turkestan. The town itself, originally laid out by the Russians eighty or a hundred years ago, is made up of broad avenues of elms and poplars running at right-angles to each other. Even before the War, at the time of my last visit, there were already a good many new buildings and now there are even more: blocks of flats, department stores, an opera, a university and an imposing new Government building. But the green avenues of tall trees are still there, and there are still enough of the old brightly painted stucco bungalows left, blue and white, pink and white, yellow and white, for the town not to have lost its pleasantly bucolic character.

What Alma Ata never has possessed and, despite the restrained orientalism of some of its new public buildings, I think never will, is anything at all Eastern in its make up. It always has been and always will be a Russian town set down in the centre of Asia. But this seems to suit the Kazak portion of the population who, forgetting their nomad past, parade up and down in their European suits looking pleased with themselves and with the amenities of their capital. In the middle of a neatly laid out and well-kept public garden a magnificent equestrian statue has been erected to the memory of a Kazak national hero who in 1916 led a revolt against the Russians and whose objectives, in theory, have now all been attained.

In front of the great new Government building, arm outstretched, little bearded chin well forward, stands an immense statue of Lenin, put up, I found, only a year ago. After thirty years of Stalinism, Lenin is coming into his own again. The statues of Stalin have for the most part not been taken down, but more and more statues of Lenin have been put up everywhere and the balance thus gradually restored. Of Khrushchov, on the other hand, I never saw a single statue in Kazakstan or anywhere else, and only a very few portraits publicly displayed. To this extent it is perhaps true that the 'cult of personality' is a thing of the past.

To suggest that the Kazaks have no say whatever in running the affairs of their own Soviet Socialist Republic would be an exaggeration. On the contrary the members of the Kazak Government and of the Alma Ata City Soviet, the Rector of the University of Kazakstan, the Chairman of the State Opera, the Director of the State Bank, the members of most of the principal commercial, industrial and agricultural enterprises in Kazakstan will on inquiry be found to be almost without exception native Kazaks. And, as far as local government is concerned, their views undoubtedly count for a good deal. There is even a Kazak Minister of Foreign Affairs, Tulegen T. Tazhibayev, though what exactly his duties can be is less clear. But, despite the decentralization which has undoubtedly taken place during the past five years, Moscow is always on the end of the telephone. The ultimate decision, the ultimate authority, the ultimate power rests with Moscow. The Party line comes from Moscow, the troops are under the command of Moscow; and for Kazakstan, as for the other Union republics, the clause in its constitution enabling it to secede voluntarily from the Union remains as totally unreal as ever.

*

The hotel to which I was escorted by the cheerful round-faced Kazak from Intourist who met me at the airport was the same one that I had managed to force my way into on my last visit, when it was newly built. Then, I had been glad to get a bed in the 'Lenin Corner' which had temporarily been converted into a dormitory and which I shared with fifteen other wayfarers. Now, as a tourist de luxe, I was shown into a de luxe suite — bedroom, sitting-room and bathroom — bright, clean, modern, plainly and rather comfortably furnished, looking out on to green trees. On the walls were several large not unpleasant Alpine landscapes in oils, and dotted about on the furniture several sizeable examples of socialist realism in bronze.

Last time I had been there I had, I remembered, had some particularly good roast duck and apple sauce. Now, twenty years later, it was again on the menu and, I found on ordering it, as good as ever. The next table to me in the hotel restaurant was a long one, laid for twenty, with an unfamiliar flag flying over it. A foreign delegation, I thought. And at that moment in came a score of Outer Mongolian women athletes, chattering to each other in Outer Mongolian and wearing different-coloured track suits. They were not unlike Kazak women to look at, but their cheekbones were higher and their cast of countenance, as one would expect, rather more Mongoloid. They had the rather agreeable carved-wooden look which most Mongols seem to have. That night at dinner they were there again, after a hard day in the stadium, eating well and drinking quantities of fizzy lemonade. But now they had changed into their national dress, a kind of

Mongolian kimono, and were wearing their jet black hair in long heavy plaits. 'How pretty that Mongolian woman athlete is,' I observed to my *sputnitsa*, pointing to one of them. 'Do you think so?' she replied.

Remembering that on my last visit I had spent two or three days climbing in the foothills of the Tien Shan, I now asked whether I could use the car that was placed at my disposal to drive up into the mountains. 'No,' came the reply, 'everything except the town itself is a forbidden zone.' But next morning, unaccountably, the car was there, waiting to take me up into the mountains as I had asked.

Almost as soon as we had left the town we started to climb steeply by a first-class new motor road which went winding up beside a rushing mountain stream along a typical Alpine valley. Here and there we passed plantations of conifers. Above us rose the snowy peaks of the Tien Shan. We might have been in Switzerland. 'There,' said my companions proudly, 'is the skating-rink we have made for the Olympic Games, but' — resentfully — 'they won't give it a trial.' They seemed to have forgotten about the forbidden zone. 'Can I photograph?' I asked. 'Certainly,' they said. Only at one moment on our way home did considerations of security impinge on my photography. 'Now you must stop photographing,' they suddenly said. And then three minutes later: 'Now you may start again.' As we passed through the forbidden zone I looked hopefully round, but there were no atomic piles or rocket-launching platforms to be seen — only a few suburban villas with vines and sunflowers growing in their gardens.

'You will,' they said, 'wish to see our Park of Rest and Culture and our Champagne Factory.' Everybody in Alma Ata had been so nice to me that I agreed. First we went to the Park of Rest and Culture. Round the entrance stood plaster statues of splendidly developed young women, playing tennis or basket-ball. At first sight they seemed to be studies in the nude. But on closer inspection I found that they were all provided with form-fitting two-piece plaster bathing-suits, which made very little difference to the general effect, but satisfied the demands of Soviet prudishness — a rather surprising characteristic of which one is constantly encountering fresh evidence. Along the asphalted alleyways under the trees flocked troops of small Kazak and Russian children, stopping from time to time to buy an ice-cream or a glass of fizzy lemonade, or to take a turn on the swings and roundabouts. Here and there were running-tracks or sports grounds on which young people of both sexes were engaging with the utmost energy in athletic pursuits of one kind or another, some panting along over a five-hundred-metre course, while others demonstrated their skill at the long jump or on the parallel bars. Near by was a lake where boating and swimming was in progress. An immense new stadium, I was told, was under construction. On the way home we passed a new language institute. Education, physical training — wherever you go in the Soviet Union you find them emphasized and exalted.

I have always believed in approaching the wines of whatever country I happen to be in with an open mind, in giving them a fair trial. It is, I think, a grave mistake to assume that drinkable wine is only grown in France and in one or two chosen areas in one or two other European countries. In the course of my travels I have drunk with pleasure the light white wines of Slovenia, the heavy sweet wine of Dalmatia, Greek retsina with its undertones of turpentine, Richon-le-Zion, the red wine of Palestine, saki, the rice wine of Japan, rakia, the plum brandy of Bosnia, the wine of Shiraz in southern Persia, which is supposed to have given its name to sherry, the delicious red, white and pink wines of the Caucasus and a number of other perfectly good local wines from different parts of Switzerland, Italy, Spain, Portugal, South Africa and Luxembourg. For all this, I must admit that the idea of a champagne factory in the Soviet Socialist Republic of Kazakstan slightly unnerved me. However, I was clearly expected to go there and so go there I did.

From the outside it looked very much like any other factory: a series of nondescript whitewashed buildings on the outskirts of the town. The proceedings began with a visit to the director in his office, an agreeable Russian, who explained the processes used in the production of champagne, processes identical with those employed in France. The grapes, he added, were from special champagne vines. I asked him if he himself had ever been to France. No, he said, not to France, though he hoped to go. But he had been abroad as a soldier during the War, and on comparing notes, we found we had fought on the same front in the Balkans. Then we started off round the factory.

Like so many things in the Soviet Union it was a mixture of the very modern and the extremely primitive. Tremendously up-to-date machinery was helped out by a number of those shapeless, motherly middle-aged Russian women with aprons and handkerchiefs round their heads, who in an emergency always seem to step into the breach and make things work by pushing and pulling, persistence and plain common sense.

Not all shapeless, though. The forewoman was tall, young, dark and handsome. She also clearly knew her job. With assurance and a wealth of technical detail she explained how the wine was made; how it was taken from the barrels and bottled; and how, left to itself, it went with the passage of time naturally and spontaneously fizzy. (I was relieved to hear this, having half suspected chemicals and gas.) After a fixed number of years, she went on, the bottles were opened, a spoonful or so of syrup made of sugar and brandy was inserted and they were corked up again, their contents thus ceasing to be '*brut*' and becoming '*sec*' or '*demi-sec*', according to the amount of syrup that went in. Would I like to try some?

What I would like to try, I said, was the *brut*, the natural wine before they put in the syrup. She seemed surprised at this, but took down a bottle from the rack and opened it. A glass was produced and I drank some. It tasted delicious: not a great wine, but a light, dry champagne, not unlike the '*champagne nature*' one finds in France. And why, after all, not? Gently sloping hillsides, fertile soil, plenty of sun, the right vines, grapes carefully picked, pressed, barrelled and bottled — there is no reason why the result should not be a perfectly sound wine. Was the *brut* ever put on the market? I asked. No, replied the beautiful forewoman, only the *sec* and the *demi-sec*. But of those the combined champagne factories of the Soviet Union produced a total of twenty-five million bottles a year.

On my way back to the hotel I stopped at a bookshop where, needing something to read, I bought a copy of *Anna Karenina*. Being snobbish about reading Russian books in English, and lacking the resolution to read them in Russian, I had never read it before. Even now I wondered whether I should really get through it, and in case it proved too much for me bought, to fall back on, a Russian translation of *The Adventures of Sherlock Holmes*, printed in Alma Ata by the Kazak State Publishing Organization. But when I got back to the hotel and lay down on my bed and began to read I found from the very start that, rusty though my Russian was, I was being carried along irresistibly by the story, and, as one after another they took shape and came to life, irresistibly involved in the destinies of the different characters.

When a couple of hours later I reluctantly closed my book and went into the restaurant to get something to eat, it was to find that the Outer Mongolian women had left and that the long table in the middle of the room was now occupied by a delegation of both sexes from East Germany, dressed in the kind of clothes which Germans wear when travelling. Some were busy eating. Others exchanged comments — serious or humorous — on the episodes and incidents of the day. Seen and heard in the mass, Germans, I have observed, are often less attractive than when encountered individually. It was with feelings of relief that, having finished my dinner, I hurried back to the silence of my room and to the fascinating, many-faceted world into which Tolstoi's novel had plunged me.

Next morning, having exhausted what the East Germans at the next table kept calling the *Sehenswürdig-keiten* of Alma Ata, I took an aeroplane back to Tashkent, hardly glancing up as we flew over the arid expanses of the Kizil Kum from the enthralling pages of *Anna Karenina*. How lucky I was, I reflected, to have had this splendid treat kept in store for me all these years; how fortunate that I had not read it before, when, being younger, I might have appreciated it less.

In Tashkent it was very, very hot. In the hotel restaurant the electric fans were whirring and the orchestra playing louder than ever. And now it appeared that the beer was running out. There was only enough left for delegations, and none for anyone else. And sure enough, while we all sat and sweltered and drank vodka or tea or tepid water, trayful after trayful of frosted bottles were brought to a group of progressive Frenchmen in a corner.

Resentment at this favouritism proved a bond with my three table companions: a young sailor in uniform and his father and mother. He, it appeared, was home on short leave from his ship and they were gazing at him adoringly. The father was an Uzbek, dark-skinned with high cheekbones and slanting eyes; the mother a fair-haired Russian with blue eyes and a pink and white complexion. Tall, good-looking and smart in his uniform, the son had his mother's blue eyes. His complexion, though sunburnt, was not very dark. Only his high cheekbones indicated his oriental descent. And now, sitting here in Tashkent a thousand miles and more from the ocean, he was telling his parents about his travels and the seas he had sailed and the foreign ports he had visited. And they sat listening to him and looking at him and plying him with food and drink and lamenting that there was no iced beer for him.

As invariably happens on a journey, I now found on taking them out of my pocket that my only pair of sun-glasses had fallen apart. Without much hope of success I asked my *sputnitsa* if she thought I could get them mended, and together we set out into the blazing afternoon sunlight to find a spectacle-repairer. At the corner of the street we found a shop with an old Russian in it mending watches. 'Can you mend these spectacles?' asked my *sputnitsa*. 'No,' said the old man without looking up, 'too busy.' 'Not even for a foreigner?' she said. 'Oh,' came the immediate reply, 'if it's for a foreigner, that's different.' And putting aside the watch he was working on he at once started looking for a screw to fit the hinge of my sun-glasses. At last he found one and with infinite care hammered it into shape. 'I must,' he kept saying as he fitted it to the hinge, 'do a job that there will be no need to be ashamed of when you take it back to Great Britain.' And when I tried to pay him, he absolutely refused to take any money.

At the hotel an American tourist was leaving for the airport. As he was going out of the door one of the hotel servants came running after him with two suits of clothes he had left in his room. But the American waved him away. 'For you! For you,' he said, smiling genially and pointing at the man, and got into the car and drove off. 'How funny Americans are!' said my *sputnitsa* sourly.

'As if we wanted their clothes!' But in fact even in Moscow foreign-made clothes are greatly prized, and the suits the American had left must have been more welcome than the most lavish tip.

I had now seen Samarkand, I had seen Alma Ata, and I had seen more than I wanted of Tashkent. But I had still not reached Bokhara. Once more I returned to the attack. It was, however, of no avail. 'No,' said the head of the Intourist office at Tashkent, 'the matter has now been referred back to Moscow and Moscow confirms my decision. Tourists may not visit Bokhara. Permits to go there are not issued by the militia. There is no way of getting there, and nothing to eat and nowhere to live when you do get there. It would not be cultured and you would not enjoy it. I have no more to say on the subject.'

This was more like old times. Up to now the readiness of the Soviet authorities to let me go anywhere I wanted and the speed and ease with which my journeys had been accomplished had rather taken the gilt off the ginger-bread. Even the advantage of being able to examine in detail and at my leisure the ancient splendours of Shakh Zindeh and the Gur Emir, and to live in comfort while I did so, could not quite replace the thrill of having got somewhere where it was hard to get to. Now I was once again faced with the old problem of how best to over-come or get round an obstacle placed in my way.

Of all the towns I had been to in Turkestan, Bokhara, as it happened, was the one I most wanted to see again. For some years past, while collecting material for a book

I was writing, I had read everything about Bokhara that I could lay my hands on. This had still further aroused my interest in it, and now I wanted to go there even more than I had twenty years before. For a time I toyed with the idea of doing what I had done once before, of simply taking a train to the nearest main-line station and then walking. Then another, better idea occurred to me.

Making my way back to Moscow — a distance of about two thousand miles — I took advantage of a convenient diplomatic reception to get myself introduced to Mr Khrushchov. It was a splendid reception. Unlike those of twenty years ago it was swarming with Russians: Ministers, marshals, musicians, officials, writers, actors, all eating and drinking and chattering away sixteen to the dozen. As for Khrushchov, he was friendliness itself. Friendliness, shrewdness and bounce. His watchful little eyes twinkled with vitality. In other circumstances, one surmised, his face might have been totally different. But for the moment it was wreathed in smiles.

Was I, he asked, enjoying my visit to the Soviet Union? Yes, I said, I was. Did I notice a difference? Yes, I said, I did. Had I seen everything I wanted to? No, I said, I hadn't. I hadn't seen the place I wanted to see most of all. I hadn't seen Bokhara. And then I proceeded to direct his attention to the unsympathetic attitude of one section of his subordinates. I was, I said, writing a book about Bokhara, and they would not let me go there. Was it not unreasonable and mean to place such obstacles in the way of a harmless historian? ('So now,' murmured a near-by Soviet official who knew me of old, 'you are a historian!') But Mr Khrushchov, no doubt anxious to conclude a conversation that threatened to become tedious, hastened to agree with everything I said. 'Yes, yes,' he said. 'Yes, yes.' In that case, I put in hurriedly, could I leave for Bokhara at once? 'Yes,' he said, moving away, 'of course, of course. But don't blame me if you're uncomfortable when you get there.' My Summit Talk had achieved its object. Forty-eight hours later I was coming in to land at Bokhara, a brilliant green patch against the tawny desolation that surrounded it.

Last time I had entered Bokhara on foot, having walked there from the main-line railway station fifteen miles away, followed by two secret policemen and a string of Bactrian dromedaries. At first I had been none too certain whether I had taken the right road. Then, from the top of a little hill, I had suddenly found myself looking down in the moonlight on the massive white walls and watchtowers of the city and, passing through one of its eleven great fortified gates, had slept that night under a bush in the garden of a mosque.*

This time I was a little bewildered as the car from the City Soviet which had met me at the airport, after traversing the orchards and fields and gardens that surround Bokhara, finally drew up outside the hotel right in the middle of the town. Subconsciously I had been looking out for the walls and gates, and had not been aware of them. Surely I could not have been so absorbed in my conversation with the charming Uzbek City Librarian who had come to meet me as not to notice them. 'Where,'

* See *Eastern Approaches*.

I asked him, 'are the walls? And the gates?' 'Oh,' he said,
'they've been knocked down.' 'The whole lot?' I asked.
'Pretty well the whole lot,' he said. 'It makes the town so
much more airy.'

And sure enough, when a little later, having deposited
my belongings in the clean little room I had been allotted
at the hotel, I set out in the blazing midday heat to re-
explore the town, I found tremendous changes. Twenty
years ago Bokhara had been a walled city, unchanged
in many respects since the days of the Emirs, indeed since
the Middle Ages. It looked as though the Russians,
despairing of ever sovietizing it, had simply left it to decay.
But now the ancient walls and gates had been swept away
and a number of wide, tree-lined, asphalted boulevards
driven through the maze of narrow winding streets and
flat-roofed mud-built houses. Many of the inhabitants
had discarded their turbans and *khalats* for modern Soviet
suits. A Park of Rest and Culture had appeared as well
as several smaller public gardens. A stadium and various
new buildings had been put up, and others were under
construction. There were even rows of neat little flat-
roofed single-storeyed dwelling-houses that looked rather
like our own prefabs. Finally, the notorious open canals,
which until not so long ago had both served as sewers
and provided drinking-water, had been replaced by an
up-to-date water system which brought in clean piped
water from the hills, and an imposing new water-tower
was now much in evidence amongst the ancient monuments. Unlikely as it had seemed on my last visit,
Bokhara was already well on the way to becoming an up-
to-date Soviet town, a new ornament of the Soviet

Socialist Republic of Uzbekistan, perhaps in due course even a tourist centre.

And yet at every step I found pointers to a prodigious and blood-stained past. Bokhara es Sherif it was formerly called, Bokhara the Noble. Elsewhere in the world, it was said, light came down from heaven; but from Bokhara light went up. 'Une cité moult noble et grant', wrote Marco Polo; and Anthony Jenkinson, an Elizabethan merchant-adventurer who made his way there in 1558, speaks of the 'great citie' with its 'high walls of earth with divers gates into the same' and its 'many houses, temples and monuments of stone sumptuously builded and gilt'. Right up to the time of the Revolution it was considered the holiest city in all Central Asia and boasted over three hundred and fifty mosques and over a hundred religious colleges and *medressehs*.

For some time past I had been piecing together the story of two British officers, Colonel Charles Stoddart and Captain Arthur Conolly, who in the first half of the nineteenth century, when Bokhara was still an independent state, were sent there as emissaries to the court of of Emir Nasrullah, and after long months of imprisonment and torture had eventually met their end there, a terrifying, solitary end, thousands of miles from home, beyond all reach of help.*

Now, with the aid of the various pieces of information I had collected, I was able to trace their tragic progress step by step from the time of their first arrival in the city. Here, for example, was the Registan, the great open space in front of the Citadel, into which Colonel Stoddart,

---

* See *A Person from England.*

wearing his cocked hat and firmly disregarding local usage, had impetuously ridden his horse on the occasion of his first visit to the Emir. And here, towering above it, was the thousand-year-old Citadel or Ark, where the Emir sat in state and where Stoddart had refused to bow down before him, hitting out angrily at a high court official who came too near him.

The Ark still stands much as it did in Stoddart's day, a massive fortress which once contained a veritable rabbit-warren of tumbledown palaces, mosques, harems and offices. Some of it, it seems, was destroyed when the last Emir set fire to it as he fled in the summer of 1920 before the rapidly advancing Red cavalry, but you may still see the antiquated telephone by which he received the fateful message warning him of their approach. The great entrance gate is flanked by twin turrets, between which hung until recently a clock made for the Emir by an Italian, Giovanni Orlandi of Parma, eventually bludgeoned to death for refusing to become a Mohammedan or, some say, for allowing the Emir's watch to stop.

You enter the Ark by a steep, dark, winding passageway flanked on either side by sinister-looking guard-rooms and torture-chambers and cells for prisoners. This was the way taken on his arrival in the city by Dr Wolff, the eccentric missionary, who in the year 1843 set out of his own accord from Richmond Green to travel thousands of miles across seas and mountains and deserts with the object of bearding the Emir in his lair and asking him to his face what he had done with Stoddart and Conolly.

Not far from the Ark rises the great glittering turquoise dome of the Kalyan Mosque where the Emir used to worship in person and where Colonel Stoddart, having been forced for a time to abjure Christianity and embrace Islam, was regularly obliged to attend prayers. High above it and above the whole of Bokhara looms the elaborately decorated twelfth-century Minari Kalyan, also known as the Tower of Death, from the top of which, under the Emirs, condemned criminals used to be thrown down.

Just behind the Ark I found after some inquiry the Zindan, or prison, where Stoddart and Conolly spent so many miserable months, partly in a low dark cell and partly in a pit, twenty-one feet deep, where the Emir kept a selection of specially bred vermin and reptiles for the express purpose of tormenting his victims, and where, we are told, 'masses of their flesh' were 'gnawed off their bones'. Today you may still see the pit, now neatly cemented, as a monument to Soviet enlightenment and to the total depravity of oriental potentates. At the bottom of it crouch two lifelike dummies, while a villainous-looking jailer in Bokharan uniform gazes vindictively down at them from above. Near by is the place where the Englishman and the Irishman, having resolutely refused to turn Mohammedan, were finally executed. To this day the tradition of the two British prisoners of the Emir lingers in Bokhara, and the names of Stoddart and Conolly, or Khan Ali as he was called, are still remembered there.

Only one religious school is now open in Bokhara and of the hundreds of mosques and *medressehs* most have long since disappeared, but a number still survive. The two biggest stand near the Tower of Death in the centre of the town: The Kalyan or Kok Gumbaz (Blue Dome) and the colossal Mir Arab, both built in the sixteenth century. Like their counterparts in Samarkand the mosques and *medressehs* of Bokhara are constructed of sunbaked bricks of different shades of pale red and brown. The design is usually the same: in the centre of the façade the central arch, or *pishtak*, reaching the whole height of the building, with, on either side, a double row of smaller arches. In the *medressehs* the central arch forms the entrance to one or more courtyards surrounded by cloisters and rows of cells. Most of the mosques in Bokhara have lost the coloured tiles which formerly adorned their façades and which are still to be seen in Samarkand: but the *medressehs* of Ulug Beg and Abdul Azis, which stand facing each other not far away from the Tower of Death, have retained at least some of their former splendour, their façades being still decorated with their original intricate arabesques. The Ulug Beg *medresseh*, like the *medresseh* of the same name in Samarkand, was built by Tamerlane's grandson, Ulug Beg the famous astronomer, in the early fifteenth century. As for the other, lesser mosques and *medressehs*, a very few are still in use; but for the most part they stand abandoned or have been turned to other uses. Of the buildings which stand round the Liabi Khaus, the tree-shaded pool in the centre of the town, the Divan Begi Mosque is now a much-frequented billiard club and the Divan Begi *medresseh* an hotel, while the local record office is housed in the Kukeldash. As for the Liabi Khaus itself, it echoes with shouts and splashes, as dozens of little Uzbek boys take headers into it.

Also near the Tower of Death is what remains of the covered bazaar, once the richest in Central Asia. Now only clusters of beehive-shaped domes are left, at the point where two or more streets intersect. Here, in mysterious recesses where rubies and emeralds and Circassian slaves once changed hands for fabulous prices, a desultory trade is now done in ice-cream and fizzy drinks. Another survival from the Middle Ages are the caravanserais, where the caravans arriving in Bokhara from the outside world once made halt before continuing on their way and where now innumerable families of Bokharans have found homes, sleeping in the surrounding cells and overflowing in the daytime into the central courtyards, formerly piled high with merchandise from China, Arabia and the Indies.

On the highest point of every one of the principal buildings in Bokhara is perched each summer a stork's nest, and for a time the air resounds with the clicking and clapping of the long yellow beaks of these engaging birds. From their points of vantage the storks watch each other and everything that goes on around them. Nobody worries them and they seem to lead a happy and contented existence.

Before I left Bokhara I decided to see what, if anything, was left of the city walls. After lengthy inquiries I finally elicited the information that the massive Karakul Gate, by which the eccentric Dr Wolff entered the city in 1844, had not yet been destroyed, and having made my way there found that in this sector the walls, too, were still standing. From where I was they stretched far away into the distance, twenty or thirty feet high, crumbling

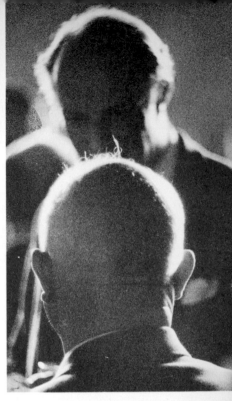

Samarkand:
'A great concourse of worshippers'

'Yes, yes', he said. 'Yes, yes.'

Bokhara. *Above:* Kalyan Mosque *Below:* The Ark

and breached, but still massive and imposing. As I stood looking at the Karakul Gate and thinking vaguely about Dr Wolff and the other travellers who had passed under it, there was a loud hoot and a three-ton truck suddenly shot out of it, crammed full of Uzbeks singing and thumping drums and bound apparently on some evening jaunt into the country. For a time their high-pitched nasal voices and the rhythmic thud of the donkey-skin drums they were pounding came echoing through the gathering darkness, and then once again there was silence.

By the time I got back to the hotel it was quite dark and still stiflingly hot. But even the greatest heat does not impair my appetite, and after changing my shirt and putting my head under a tap in the hotel washroom I strolled down the street to see what I could get to eat at what I had been told was the most 'cultured' restaurant in Bokhara.

When in doubt in the Soviet Union I usually order Bœuf Stroganov, a dish called after an early Siberian empire builder, who presumably lived on it while exploring and colonizing Siberia. It consists of chopped beef cooked with fried onions and sour cream. I have never known it turn out really badly and it is often excellent. This time it had fried potatoes with it and was particularly good.

By now I was very thirsty. Was there any beer? I asked. No, said the waitress, only tea and champagne. I had already drunk Kazak champagne, so why not Uzbek, however incongruous it might sound? When it came it was well iced and perfectly drinkable. After finishing my champagne and eating some apples and some apricots and some cherries and half a tumbler of sour cream, I was still very thirsty. I accordingly ordered some Bokharan green tea. It came in a very large pot with a very small bowl to drink it out of. It is a most refreshing drink and I sat there drinking it and smoking some remarkably good Bulgarian cigarettes until it was time to go to bed.

But although it was time to go to bed it was still, in fact, much too hot to think of doing anything of the kind. Instead, I strolled amid a dense flood of townspeople doing the same thing down the principal street, and on past the great mosques and the Tower of Death to where the Ark stood grim, white and massive in the moonlight. From the little public park which now fringes the Registan came sounds of music, and there in the darkness under the trees a crowd had gathered watching while a young Russian played the accordion and two of his friends, kicking out their legs and springing in the air, danced a Cossack dance on the gravel and everyone else clapped and beat time to the music. Then the two men sat down and two girls took their place, the tune changing as they glided gracefully through the intricate movements of the *Lezghinka*. And so it went on until there was no one left to dance, and the accordionist stopped playing, and singly or in pairs we drifted off through the empty streets to bed.

Next morning the sun was blazing and it was hotter than ever. By now my *sputnitsa* was beginning to feel the strain, the city librarian had returned to his library, and so, having first provided myself with a map, I set out on my own to look for two or three ancient monuments which I had not yet been able to locate. But I was not left by myself for long. Seeing me looking at a map two tiny brown Uzbek boys of about eight with shaven heads and very little on, but both strangely enough wearing large shiny wrist-watches, immediately came up and asked me what I was trying to do. 'To find,' I said, 'the Char Minar.' 'Right,' they squeaked. 'Follow us.' And, scampering on ahead, led me at a brisk pace through a labyrinth of winding lanes to the mosque I was looking for, a strange structure built in the early eighteenth century and bearing, as its name indicates, four bulbous blue-tiled minarets. 'We can spare you no more time,' they said briskly as soon as we arrived, and having consulted their watches vanished as suddenly as they had appeared.

My other two objectives, the shrine of Chasma Ayub and the mausoleum of Ismael Samani, I finally found beyond the Park of Rest and Culture, standing near each other on some waste land on the outskirts of the town, odd-looking, biscuit-coloured buildings of great antiquity. The shrine of Chasma Ayub, or Job's Spring, was built, it appears, by Tamerlane on the site of a miraculous spring which gushed forth there many centuries before at the behest of the prophet Job; its most distinctive feature is a strange sugar-loaf tower. The mausoleum of Ismael Samani, a squat domed building ornamented with elaborate designs in brickwork, was built by the founder of the Samanid dynasty in the ninth century A.D.

Bokhara has always been famous for its gold-embroidered caps and waistcoats, and on my last day there I asked if I could see where they were made. After walking for some distance through narrow winding lanes between high windowless mud walls, we came to a rambling kind

of house consisting of a number of long low rooms opening on to a courtyard with a tree growing in the middle.
Here a hundred or more native girls were at work, stitch-
ing and embroidering either by hand or with machines.
In another part of the building a dozen Bokharan men
were hammering away for all they were worth at ornamental brass plates, while a very old man in a turban
with a long white beard sat cross-legged on the ground
drawing the designs for them on a sheet of paper. By his
side stood the inevitable pot of refreshing green tea.

I was shown round by the director of the *Artelj*, or
Guild, an efficient and energetic Uzbek who, happening
to meet me that evening while strolling in the street,
insisted on buying me an ice-cream, saying that he felt
sure I must be terribly bored in so small a town. I was in
fact anything but bored. I had enjoyed every moment of
my stay in Bokhara. The good food in the restaurant and
the friendliness and anxiety to please of all concerned
made up for the heat, the flies, the lack of plumbing and
any other minor inconveniences. For me, despite the degree
of modernization which it has undergone, Bokhara still
retains, and will continue to retain, much of its old
fascination.

As I flew in an ordinary low-flying twin-engined aircraft from Tashkent to Tiflis on my way back to Moscow,
Central Asia unfolded itself before me as though in a
diorama. The weather was threatening when we took off
from Tashkent and the piled-up thunderclouds promised
a bumpy flight over the desert. Soon we had crossed the

Jaxartes and were over the pale, reddish-brown expanse
of the Kizil Kum — the Red Sands; then came two or
three ranges of sandstone hills, and, leaving Samarkand
behind on the left, we flew along the valley of the Zeraf-
shan, the Gold Bearer. '*Bukhara!*' said the exceptionally
pretty Uzbek air-hostess, ivory skinned, sleek-haired and
trim in a neat black skirt and well-filled pink and white
candy-striped blouse. And there it was once more, with
its crumbling walls, domes and minarets, pale and dead-
looking under the gun-metal glare of the sky. Then a
strip of desert again, and then the broad muddy stream
of the Oxus. And after that once more the desert, stretching away in every direction as far as the eye could reach.
Suddenly the sun came out in a blue sky with only a few
fleecy white clouds. Looking down I could see to the south
unexpected patches of green — the swamps where the
Murghab River runs away into the sand — and I knew
that beyond them in the heat haze lay Merv — Merv,
the oldest of all cities, once called Merou Shahou Jehan,
Merv Queen of the World, and now a heap of crumbling
ruins. But already on the horizon the blue barrier of the
Persian Mountains was emerging from the mist, rising
range upon range into the distance, and a few minutes
later we were landing at Askabad, the capital of Turkmenistan, a typical Russian Central Asian town: low
white houses in wide green avenues running at right-
angles to each other. The heat and glare were terrific.
At the airport the bunches of grapes hanging from the
ornamental trellis were almost ripe. The buzz of flies in
the buffet was a warning to keep out. Turkomans in blue
overalls squatted cross-legged in the rare patches of shade.

At the local theatre they were giving *The Merry Widow*. It seemed a shame to miss it. But by now we were back in the aircraft; a fat Turkoman woman waved a white flag; and we flew off again westwards along the line of the railway. Beneath us now was Gök Tepe, the last stronghold of the Tekke Turkomans, stormed by General Skobelyov on the twenty-fourth of January, 1881. To the south, a dozen or so miles away, the mountains marked the Persian frontier. To the north lay the wide plain across which the panic-stricken fugitives fled before Skobelyov's pursuing Cossacks, who massacred them by thousands, men, women and children alike. The desert was now no longer reddish-brown but of a different colour: a bleak blackish-grey, inexpressibly dreary and dismal under the blazing sun: the Kara Kum, the Black Sands. After a time the monotony was broken first by one mountain range rising abruptly from the plain and then by another: the Greater and the Lesser Balkan, round which just ninety-five years ago the Hungarian traveller, Arminius Vambery had skirted on his way to Khiva, disguised as a dervish.

Suddenly we caught sight of the sea. The port of Krasnovodsk lay spread out beneath us with the long sandy coastline stretching away on either side. And in a few minutes we had left Central Asia behind us and were flying far out over the blue-green waters of the Caspian.

THREE

DEEP SOUTH

'THERE are,' they told me in reply to my inquiry, 'no Teddy boys in Tashkent.' 'But,' they said, 'just wait till you get to Tiflis!' I did, and I was not disappointed. The Teddy boys in Tiflis are quite something. *Stilyagi,* they call them in Russian — the stylish ones — which perhaps explains why they flourish so in the agreeable capital of the Soviet Socialist Republic of Georgia.

The Georgians, wine-drinkers, true southerners and at the same time true highlanders, have an excitable nature, a generous, sunny disposition and a tremendous natural sense of style. They enjoy making a noise. They enjoy fighting. They enjoy dressing up. And they enjoy showing off. From the moment you arrive in their beautiful sunlit country with its splendid mountains, its vineyards and its ancient stone-built villages and towns, you cannot help being struck by how handsome the inhabitants are: the men with their proud bearing and fierce hawklike good looks; the women darkly beautiful with their flashing eyes, aquiline features and slender pliant bodies. Already, before we had left Central Asia, I noticed several typical Georgians at Tashkent Airport queuing for the Tiflis aeroplane. Gesticulating and laughing they stood out from the rest of the waiting crowd and, even before we were completely airborne, they were out of their seats and joking and flirting with the pretty airhostess.

As a race the Georgians are by nature less serious, less hard-working, more elegant and more mercurial than the Russians. Even under a Soviet regime they manage to retain an agreeable Ruritanian flavour. After all, as recently as 1920 it was calculated that at least one in seven of the population were princes. It is perhaps scarcely surprising that in Tiflis the national taste for style and display should in these latter days have manifested itself in a proportionately larger number of Teddy boys than are to be found in other Soviet cities.

The hotel to which I was taken from Tiflis Airport was the old Orient, where I had stayed in 1938, and where my grandfather, incidentally, had stayed while on a visit to Transcaucasia fifty years before. In the long, cool, vaulted dining-room luncheon was being served when I arrived. The tall French windows stood open; sun-blinds kept out the glare and bustle of the street. I was tired and hungry after the long flight from Tashkent and was glad when Vakhtang, the incredibly sauve mustachioed *maître d'hôtel*, so called after the legendary Georgian hero of that name, brought me the menu and a small carafe of iced vodka. He could, he said, strongly recommend two Georgian dishes, *sungun* and *liulia kebab*, and a bottle of *Tsinandali*, the local white wine. *Sungun*, when it arrived, turned out to be rather a good Welsh rarebit, while *liulia kebab* was a *kebab* of grilled lamb wrapped in crisp, paper-thin Georgian bread. After that I had some strawberries and half a tumbler of *smetana*, or sour cream. The *Tsinandali* was chilled and reminded me of a light Chablis.

After luncheon I went up to my suite. It consisted of a

Bokhara: The Tower of Death   *Below:* The Vermin Pit

Bokhara.   *Above:* The Karakul Gate   *Below:* The Covered Bazaar

sizeable bedroom with a bed that was covered with frills of white lace, a bathroom and a drawing-room that was as large as a medium-sized ballroom and decorated accordingly. From the tall velvet-curtained windows I looked across to a majestic new building which since my last visit had appeared on the opposite side of the main street: the seat of the Government of Georgia.

Tiflis is a pleasant town. It lies on the banks of the Kura, a rushing mountain river. A great hill, St David's Mount, rises steeply above it. In the old parts of the town the houses, with their carved projecting balconies, cling to the precipitous hillside like swallows' nests, and the cobbled streets are almost perpendicular. Above them stands the ancient fortress, now a ruin. Many of the old churches, with their characteristic conical steeples, are still in use. Stalin's mother, old Mrs Djugashvili, who died at an advanced age in 1937, was not only extremely devout but of great force of character, and thanks to her influence the Orthodox Church was, even before the War, a good deal less savagely persecuted in Georgia than in most parts of the Soviet Union.

On Sunday morning church bells were ringing out all over the town. The singing in the cathedral, the seventh-century Sionski Sobor, was magnificent and the members of the congregation younger than is usual in the Soviet Union, and more smartly dressed. When we came out there were whole families, grandparents, parents and children standing about after the service and gossiping with their friends, much as congregations do on a Sunday anywhere. I also visited the principal Armenian church, where I was proudly shown a kind of diocesan magazine containing photographs of the Archibishop of Canterbury and of Mr Gulbenkian.

Since my last visit the seminary in which Stalin himself was once trained as an Orthodox priest had, I found, stopped being the Palace Hotel and become the Museum of Art. I spent a happy morning wandering round it. It contains a magnificent collection of early ikons, some very enjoyable eighteenth- and early nineteenth-century Georgian and Russian portraits and family groups, mainly of members of the Bagratid dynasty, some strange, rather decadent pictures painted in the nineteen-twenties by a school of young Georgian artists under French influence, and a fascinating display of photographs and plaster casts from churches in different parts of Georgia dating as far back as the fourth century. The latter filled me with an immediate desire to spend a month or two studying ecclesiastical architecture in the remote valleys of the Caucasus. How pleasant, I thought, to pursue in such spectacularly beautiful surroundings the gradual transition which in those early centuries of our era took place from the classical to the medieval.

In Tiflis, as in so many southern cities, there is an agreeable tradition that towards sundown the greater part of the population stop doing whatever they are supposed to be doing and meet to stroll till far into the night in twos and threes slowly up and down the principal street of the town, looking at each other and exchanging greetings and gossip. One side, I was told, was much smarter than the other. It is here — on the smarter side of the street —

that the Teddy boys of Tiflis may be seen in all their glory. By what mysterious international telepathy have the fashions and tastes of the Tottenham Court Road communicated themselves to Transcaucasia, I wondered, as I watched the simpler youths parading in their tartan shirts and slacks, while the more sophisticated displayed the full regalia of crew-cut, drainpipe trousers, draped jackets, string ties and rubber-soled shoes. 'Why are you photographing me?' asked one of them as I brought my movie camera to bear on him. 'Because,' I replied, 'you are wearing such an exceptionally elegant suit.' And at once his expression of momentary concern was replaced by a self-satisfied smirk.

But despite the similarity of dress the Georgian Teds have a bolder, a more robust look than their opposite numbers in this country, and one is reminded that it was in the streets of Tiflis that a couple of years ago took place something unheard of in the Soviet Union: a public riot — the reaction of the younger generation of Georgian patriots to the insults heaped posthumously by Khrushchov on Stalin, the local boy who made good and who is now a good deal more popular in his native country than he ever was in his lifetime. 'They are terrible nationalists, the Georgians,' said an old Russian to me as we watched the passers-by in the street. 'It's all Georgian this and Georgian that. Always has been and always will be.' And he spat expressively on the pavement.

It is extraordinary what a difference silk stockings and high-heeled shoes make to a girl's appearance. Twenty years ago both were practically unobtainable in the Soviet Union. Now, in Tiflis, half the girls in the street were wearing them. I noticed, too, as I strolled along the street, how busy the hairdressers and manicurists were kept. At ten o'clock at night their shops were still invariably open and completely filled with customers having their hair done and their finger-nails and toe-nails manicured and varnished. Another thing that struck me was the number of ground-floor windows in which were exhibited little notices advertising private dressmakers and embroideresses and, as often as not, displaying examples of their wares. PLISSÉS, said the notices whatever *plissés* are. Jewellery, too, is coming back and is now worn more and more by anyone with any pretensions to smartness. Georgian girls are clearly conscious of their good looks and determined to make the best of them. Nor is it only the young people who take pains with their appearance. Again and again I met smart little old ladies tripping along the street dressed up to the nines, like aunts at a garden party, and even wearing hats, a thing that in pre-war years was unheard of.

Other characteristics of the Georgians that constantly find expression in the street are excitability, hot temper and a natural tendency to dramatize. Twice in half an hour in the main street of the town, among the strolling crowds, I watched a conversation turn into an argument and an argument develop into a free fight. In both instances the victim was a man and the aggressor a woman, who fell on him literally tooth and nail, drawing blood copiously in the first few seconds. And on both occasions the crowd immediately gathered round, cheering on the combatants and cheering the single harassed policeman who, when he tried to intervene, got his face scratched and his shins kicked for his pains and was finally obliged to

Above: Job's Spring   *Below:* The Walls of Bokhara

Bokhara: Char Minar

'A very old man in a turban'

summon reinforcements by means of a series of agonized blasts on his whistle.

Photography, especially motion-photography, was, I found, full of hazards in Tiflis. Most Georgians adore being photographed. As soon as the whirr of a ciné-camera is heard, heads appear at windows, people shout, children come running up, a crowd assembles. 'Me! Me!' they yell. 'Photograph me, little grandfather.' Then, as you take aim, a baby starts crying, someone pushes some-one else, chickens run squawking from under their feet, blows are exchanged, and in a matter of seconds mayhem has broken out.

Only once did the police intervene. Happening to look up from my camera as I was photographing in the back streets of the old town, I saw two uniformed figures stand-ing at my side. Both had white tunics, with scarlet facings and brass buttons, hawklike noses and little black moustaches. 'What,' they inquired simultaneously in broken Russian, 'are you doing?' 'Photographing,' I replied. 'Why?' they said. 'Why not?' I replied. 'It is forbidden by law,' they said. 'No, it isn't,' I said, produc-ing a book of by-laws which I happened to have in my pocket. 'Who,' they retorted, 'are you?' 'A tourist,' I replied. 'Ah,' they said, 'a tourist — a guest, a guest of Georgia.' And then: 'Do you like our country?' 'Very much indeed,' I replied. 'I,' said one, 'am a Georgian.' 'And I,' said the other, 'am an Armenian.' In return I explained what I was. 'And how,' asked the Georgian, 'is Churchill, the friend of Our Stalin? Is he quite all right? Has he got a pension, a big enough pension?' I assured him that Sir Winston was suffering no hardship. 'And

are there,' asked the Armenian excitedly, 'many Arme-
nians in Great Britain?' I said that there were quite a lot.
At this he laughed delightedly. 'I bet they're doing well,'
he said. 'I bet that by now they're all lords,' '*Vsye Lordovi!*'
he went on repeating: 'All lords.' 'Is it all right now for
me to photograph?' I asked as we parted. 'Of course!
Of course! Photograph! Photograph!' they said and
flapped their hands at me affirmatively. 'Can I photograph
you?' I asked. 'No,' they replied. 'we're a secret,' and made
off as fast as they could go.

Before the War I had taken the funicular up to the top
of St David's Mount to look at the view. This time, feeling
the need for exercise, I walked up, climbing at sunset
up through the steeply inclined cobbled streets of the
old town and then on by a precipitous mountain track
to the top. Half-way up was the ancient church of St
David and a small cemetery in which Stalin's mother lies
buried. Pausing there on my way up I found two air
force officers searching diligently for her tomb. 'Where
is it?' they asked anxiously.

It had been a stiff climb, and by the time I reached
the top it was getting late and I felt ready for some
refreshment. Since my last visit the whole summit of
the mountain had, I found, been laid out as a Stalin Park
of Rest and Culture with gravel paths, flower-beds and a
great statue of the dead dictator wearing his winter
greatcoat. In the middle of all this stood a massive building containing a restaurant, with a loggia looking out over
Tiflis. This was just what I was looking for. I went in.
Far below, in the city, it was quite dark and everywhere
the lights were beginning to come out.

Even by present-day Soviet standards the decoration of that restaurant was lavish. There were bigger gilt chandeliers, there was more marble and canary-coloured plush than I had ever seen in my life before. There was a band playing. The lighting was brilliant and the customers were as merry as they could be. 'Champagne!', they shouted '*Shampanskoye!*' — and it was all the fast-scuttling, white-coated waiters could do to keep them supplied. Already toasts were being drunk from one table to another across the room, a dashing young Georgian air force officer in an immensely smart uniform giving the lead. At a large corner-table six more splendid Georgians, each with his arm round a girl's waist, were singing a traditional Caucasian folk-song which bore no relation whatever to the tune that was being played by the band. Out in the middle of the room a quiet-looking elderly man was waltzing solemnly all by himself without a partner, spinning first one way and then the other, while from the near-by tables they cheered and clapped. Meanwhile, in and out of the tables, back and forth through the swing doors, on to the dais where the band was playing, in and out between the instruments and off the other side, chased at full speed a horde of small children, all yelling as only Georgian children can. The noise was indescribable, but the atmosphere was undeniably gay, and my dinner, when it came, was delicious. Feeling pleasurably refreshed I walked down the hill to bed.

The longer I spent in Tiflis the more I liked it. Even the delegation of East German footballers, lanky brown-skinned, tow-haired youths, who for a day or two crowded out the hotel restaurant and who a generation earlier would no doubt have adorned the Hitler Jugend or the S.S., could not disturb my equanimity. When I had nothing better to do I sat on a bench in the sun in the old Alexander Gardens near the hotel, reading *Anna Karenina*, talking to anyone who talked to me and listening to the singing which came from the near-by church of St Nicholas or to the cheerful tunes which issued from the loud-speakers that hung in what once had been a bandstand. Or else I strolled through the streets looking at the shops and the houses and the churches and the people.

'What,' asked the head of Tiflis Intourist, a sallow, intelligent, uneasy-looking man, 'do you want to see now?' It is important, as a tourist in the Soviet Union, to know what you want to see; you will probably not be shown it, but if you are sufficiently persistent and make enough fuss you will in the end be shown something else as a consolation prize, which will often turn out to be much more enjoyable than your original objective. And so I had my answer ready. 'Hill sheep,' I said.

From his expression I could see that it was going to be no good. Hill sheep were not the sort of thing you showed to tourists. Unless, of course, they asked to see something else.

'Hill sheep,' he said, 'are difficult.'

'Why are they difficult?'

'Because they are in the hills. In the high, high hills.'

This gave me an opening. 'No,' I said, 'Not in the high, high hills. At this time of year they are on their way up to the hills. I know because I have seen them.

Twenty-one years ago to a day I saw them by the thousand being driven up the Georgian Military Road. And this year the spring has come much, much later.'

'The spring, it is true, is late this year. But storms have swept the road away. All along the Georgian Military Road there have been landslides. It is blocked, I am sorry to say, at half a dozen different points. We have been reluctantly obliged to close it to traffic. No, hill sheep, I fear, are difficult.'

'In that case I wish to see the Georgian Minister of Agriculture. He, I am certain, will arrange for me to see hill sheep. Hill sheep, I have been told, are the pride of Georgian agriculture.'

'Unfortunately the Minister never receives tourists. Now, if you had been a politician ... '

'But I am a politician. I have been one for years and years.'

'To us you are a tourist, a tourist de luxe. It will be difficult for you to see the Minister. Or the sheep. But,' with a bright smile, 'we will show you something else: a champagne factory, a tea-packing plant, a child welfare centre, Stalin's birthplace, a film studio.'

A Georgian film studio ... This sounded promising. The hill sheep had served their purpose. 'I am prepared, if you insist,' I said, 'to be shown a film studio.'

There are, in my experience, two kinds of sights in the Soviet Union: the ones you walk rapidly round in half an hour, listening to a monotonous rigmarole of statistics and propaganda; and the ones you somehow get inextricably mixed up in, leaving them, perhaps hours, perhaps days later, full of strange food and drink, having made numerous lifelong friends and given numerous promises to return next year when everything will be even bigger and better than it is now.

The studios of Gruzia Film, the Georgian State Film Company, fell into the second category. Drifting in through a side door I suddenly found myself face to face with a rather startled-looking family party sitting round a table having a meal. There were two or three grown-ups and a remarkably intelligent-looking little girl of about ten. Then I noticed the klieg lights, the cameras and the sound apparatus, and made a hasty withdrawal. But, 'Come in, come in,' they all said, knocking off filming and clustering round me, and then, seeing that I was carrying a ciné-camera of my own; 'What make is it? size? What lenses have you got? Show us your light-meter.'

A few minutes later I was installed side by side with the chief camera-man and, with much valuable professional advice from all sides, was making my own private film of the scene that was being played before us. It was, it appeared, out of a children's film that was to be called *Manana*, the story of a little girl who having become a famous child violinist took for one reason or another to telling fibs. Fibs that led, in turn, to complications requiring many thousand feet of film to bring them to a happy ending.

The principal part was played by a little Georgian girl called Nanuli Saradjishvili. Until a month before she had never done any acting. Then a talent scout, on the look-out for a child to play this particular part, had spotted her at her school. She had been given an audition.

The director had at once seen that she possessed exceptional gifts. Now, after a month, they found that they had
discovered not just an adequate child to take the part but
an infant prodigy, a born actress. Already her fame had
spread. Already other directors were after her. But,
they said proudly, she was acting for them, for Gruzia
Film.

Fascinated, I sat, sometimes filming, sometimes just
watching, while Nanuli acted her part — understanding
not a word that was spoken, for it was in Georgian, but
catching every shade of meaning from her timing, her
gestures, her movements and the warmth and changing
expression of her funny little face. It was perfectly true.
What they had here was something exceptional, something quite out of the ordinary.

She was not a very pretty little girl, a rather peaky
child with a sallow skin and the pronounced features of
her race, which she had not yet grown up to. But it was a
face that shone with natural intelligence, and her enormous dark eyes had a depth and a variety of expression
that I had never before seen in a child. The part suited
her. She was, after all, herself an infant prodigy and she
knew how an infant prodigy should behave. As she
scraped soundlessly away at her dummy violin her face
wore the dreamy, abstracted expression of true genius.
Next, explaining to her gullible grandparents her failure
to appear at school, she boldly launched into a flood of
dramatic narrative, describing with a truly Georgian
wealth of gesture the appalling dangers that had threatened
her. Then, as she extricated herself from one after
another of the difficulties into which her fibs had got

her, she registered in turn disingenuousness, hurt feelings, temper, hastily assumed charm, inward pleasure at the success of her stratagems, or embarrassed realization that for once she had overstepped the mark. On her father, a sea-captain who only came home between cruises, she lavished all her wiles, dancing with childish allurements a special little Georgian dance for him and lying doggo with an expression of angelic innocence when he came to see if she was in bed and asleep.

Nanuli, the delighted *régisseur* told me, had practically created the role for herself, making the most valuable suggestions and actually teaching herself the *gandagan*, a most advanced and complicated dance usually only executed by grown-up young ladies. She was, said the distinguished Shakespearian actor and actress who played her grandparents and who both bore the coveted title of People's Artist, a pleasure to act with. Her grandfather, they said, had been the famous Georgian Tenor, Vario Saradjishvili. She was following in his distinguished footsteps.

Looking at her with a father's practised eye it took me no time at all to see that she was making rings round the lot of them, both on the set and off it. 'Do you like acting, Nanuli?' I asked her. 'Yes,' she replied, looking engaging, 'I do.' And why not? I thought, as her mother, an elegant but tired-looking lady in a neat grey tailor-made with a black velvet collar, took her away to her dinner after first muffling her up in a series of woollies and wraps to prevent her from catching cold.

What else would I like to see? asked my new friends, flocking round me and admiringly fingering my

136

ciné-camera. There was, they said, an historical film called *Fatima* being made on one of the sets outside. Would it interest me to see that? Yes, I said.

Picking our way in the hot sunlight in and out of a series of barnlike buildings we eventually emerged into an open space where a Georgian mountain village had sprung into being. Stone-built huts clustered round a central keep. A couple of bored-looking horses swished their tails to keep off the flies. Under a tree stood an extremely pretty girl in Georgian national dress, looking none too pleased, while a bulky man in a white linen suit, horn-rimmed glasses, a loud tie and a panama hat straddled a rather flimsy-looking chair and poured out an unceasing flood of noisy Georgian at everyone in sight.

When he had finished they started filming again. A tall, fine-looking fellow in an immense sheepskin busby strode forward and impetuously seized the leading lady in his arms.

It was at this moment that the baby bear intervened. Quietly emerging from under a chair to which he had been tethered by a long piece of rope, he advanced on the leading man and wrapped himself and his rope affectionately round his legs, thus causing him to lose his balance and let go of the heroine. At once there were shouts of indignation from all sides, the cameras stopped whirring, and half a dozen actors, cameramen and extras rushed at the bear. But the bear, though small, was not so easily put off. Emitting a deep fierce growl worthy of a much bigger beast, he stood his ground nobly and made as if to bite the first person who dared touch him. By the time he had at last been disentangled and coaxed back to his place underneath the chair the sun had gone in, and they had to wait until it came out again to begin filming.

My friends now took advantage of this lull in the proceedings to introduce me all round. 'Here,' they said, 'is a Scotch photographer who is interested in our work.' I could have had no better introduction. Everybody was charming to me. Seen from close-to the leading lady was even lovelier than I had supposed. The great impresario was affability itself. My fellow camera-men welcomed me as a colleague. The extras, a score of dark-eyed maidens and mustachioed mountaineers, flocked round me asking questions. And, finally, when nobody was looking, the baby bear once more emerged from his temporary kennel to see what was going on. By the time they began filming again I was installed amongst the other camera-men, making my own private record of the proceedings, which became more and more dramatic as the story went on.

By now I had become so interested in everything and everybody I had seen that I asked if I could come back again next day. 'Of course,' they said. 'Then you will be able to meet our director, and he will arrange for you to be shown some of our recent films.'

George Gigolashvili, the director of Gruzia Film, was a friendly, dark little man, very intuitive and quick, who had been in the film industry all his life, except for the war years, which he had spent as Intelligence officer to a Soviet infantry battalion fighting the Germans in the mountains of the Northern Caucasus. They had, he said, had a rough time and to this day he could not bear the sight of mutton, which they had lived on exclusively — and lucky to get that. (Hill sheep, I thought.) He then asked me whether I had been in the War and what regiment I had served in. I told him: infantry too, the Cameron Highlanders. 'Ah,' he said, 'I remember that very regiment, when I was a child after the First War, during the Allied intervention, marching through Tiflis with their pipes and drums — very like the pipes and drums we have in our own mountains. But then you were on the wrong side.'

Would he, I asked him, thinking it better to change the subject, tell me about Gruzia Film? This was the first film studio I had ever been inside, in the Soviet Union or anywhere else, and I was fascinated by what I had seen. How long had it been going? What sort of films did they make for the most part?

Gruzia Film, said George, had been founded as far back as 1921, since when it had made about one hundred and fifty films. He himself had been with them since 1935 and had been director since 1954. Their present studios, which had grown up gradually, were now much too small and cramped for them and they were building properly planned new studios on a site outside the town, five or six times the size of the present ones. And he proudly displayed the magnificent new plans. In the main, he went on, they made films about Georgia. They were lucky to have within easy reach magnificent scenery and splendid-looking people.

At this moment we were joined, most appropriately, by the leading lady of *Fatima*, now extremely smart in her everyday clothes and looking as beautiful off the set as she did on it. Her name was Tamara Kokova. She was twenty-one or two years old, a Kabardinka from the republic of Karbardinia in the Central Caucasus. Though she spoke both Russian and Georgian her native tongue was Kabardinian — a language, it seemed, that was entirely unlike any other in the world. She had, she told me, wanted to be an actress all her life and had gone straight from school to a five-year course at the State Institute of Theatrical Art in Moscow. Now she was back again in her native Caucasus. She was the eldest of the family. Her younger brother and sister were still at home in Karbardinia. She had made her first film in 1955 and was now for the first time playing the lead. It was a moment she had always longed for. At last she had a part that she could really let herself go in.

As I sat listening to her and looking at her, I could not help reflecting on the advantages of mountain races over dwellers in the plain. Tall, slender and pliant, she had the proud bearing and natural grace of movement of the true highlander. With her classical beauty of feature, her white skin and her jet-black hair, she might have come from the west coast of Scotland or from Ireland. And this Celtic look was enhanced by the varying moods that were reflected in her changing expression, now animated, now sad, now pensive. With these looks, and with the dramatic talents I could see she possessed, what a success any films she made would have abroad, if they ever got there. And then there were the men, those splendid shaggy-hatted brigands I had seen on the set. With the mountains and valleys of Georgia for a background and Georgia's romantic bloodstained story for a theme, I felt like starting work on the script myself straight away.

Have any of your films ever been shown abroad, I

asked George Gigolashvili — in Great Britain for instance?
Yes, he said, he thought they had, but he was not very
sure where or when. Probably at some film festival, he
thought. But he did not seem very certain.

That evening, as I walked back to the hotel after a
private showing of some of the films they had produced,
my enthusiasm for Georgian films and film stars was still
undiminished. To start with, like most of the other Soviet
films I had seen this time, they no longer had any particular ideological slant, which in itself was a relief. The
photography, like almost all Soviet photography, was
excellent. The plots which dealt for the most part with
such perennial themes as love and war were perhaps
rather simple. Faint heart, they gave one to understand,
never won fair maid. But that made a pleasant change.
And the scenery and acting, the acting of a race of
naturally dramatic temperament, were superb.

'And now what do you want to see?' said the man
from Intourist, a little shocked to find that I was once
again loafing about and looking at nothing in particular.
'Would you like us to show you the Georgian State tea-
packing plant?' 'No,' I replied, 'I should not. I should
like to see Stalin's birthplace, and on the way there we
will stop at Mtzkhet, the ancient capital of Georgia.'
'You might also take in a collective farm,' he said plead-
ingly. 'All right,' I said, 'if you like.' And then, not
wishing to let him have it all his own way: 'Preferably a
collective hill farm, where I could see some of those hill
sheep we were talking about.'

Stalin was born at Gori, a little town in the Kura Valley about fifty miles north-west of Tiflis. Mtzkhet, which until the end of the fifth century A.D. was capital of the ancient kingdom of Georgia but is now no more than a village, lies a little off the main road which leads there — at the confluence of the Kura and Aragvi rivers, at the point where the Georgian Military Highway branches off northwards through the mountains of the main Caucasus range. The road was excellent and it did not take us long to cover the dozen or so miles which separate Mtzkhet from Tiflis.

I had passed Mtzkhet twice before, on my way across the Georgian Military Highway, but on neither occasion had I succeeded in inducing the lorry in which I was travelling to stop and let me look at it. Now, with a car at my disposal I could do as I liked, and, having made an early start, spent the morning looking at the various ancient buildings which still adorn it. Of these by far the finest is the cathedral of Sveti Tzkhoveli, built in the fourth century on the site of a miraculous tree from which on its being struck by St Nina, a fountain of oil is said to have gushed, the miracle being subsequently repeated at annual intervals on the first of October. Here, too, the vestment of Christ was found, having been brought from Golgotha by a Jew.

The present church is for the most part of fifteenth-century construction. It is built of golden-coloured stone round a central sugar-loaf steeple. Its four façades are decorated with intricate carved patterns and designs. All round it runs a high crenellated fortified wall, beyond which blue hills may be seen in the distance. In the grassy precincts of the cathedral some peasants were making hay while innumerable swallows wheeled and circled above them. Inside the cathedral, which is still in use, are buried the kings of Georgia right down to George XIII Bagration, the last king, who abdicated in favour of the Tsar of Russia in 1801. You may also still see there the font in which they were baptized.

Not far from the cathedral is the Convent of Samtavro once the home of St Nina. Here, too, is a church also dating back to the fourth century and containing the tomb of Tsar Miriam, the first Christian King of Georgia, who died in 326. Just outside Mtzkhet, perched high on a rock above the road, is all that remains of Harmotsika, the ancient citadel of the Georgian kings, today a crumbling ruin. After I had climbed the hill to look at it, we continued on our way.

Like Harmotsika, the citadel at Gori, destroyed by the Persians in the seventeenth century, is also a crumbling ruin. But right across it in red neon lights are written in Georgian the words LONG LIVE STALIN. Superficially, at any rate, Gori has not yet been de-Stalinized. There is an immense Stalin Museum containing a series of vast rooms with nothing much in them except some fanciful and artistically extremely inferior pictures of Stalin at various stages of his career. And then, of course, there is the little flat-roofed hut in which Stalin was born. This consists of two sparsely furnished whitewashed rooms, each about ten feet square, and a veranda. One room, it seems, was occupied by the landlord and the other by Stalin's father and mother. The whole structure has now been enclosed in a magnificent pillared marble pavilion with a glass roof and a neat little public garden laid out in front of it.

But although this shrine is still, up to a point, a place of pilgrimage it is no longer quite the place of pilgrimage it was. This ideological and historical fact was brought home to me when lunchtime came round. On our way into Gori I had noticed a large and most promising-looking new hotel, lavishly built, like the museum, in an up-to-date Soviet version of medieval Georgian style. This, I thought, is just the place to have lunch. And so, having spent some minutes inspecting the Stalin Museum and Stalin's childhood home, I went and hammered at the door of the hotel which, surprisingly, was shut and locked.

At length the door was grudgingly opened by an elderly hall porter, who, I noticed, had been busy playing backgammon with a second identical hall porter. The inside of the hotel was worthy of the outside. The entrance looked like a stage set for the third act of *Scheherazade*. Octagonal marble columns with bronze and gilt capitals supported a vaulted ceiling. In the background a marble staircase with a wrought iron balustrade led to what was presumably the bedroom floors. But the velvet-draped windows were, I noticed, tightly shuttered and the whole place seemed as dead as a doornail.

'Lunch?' I said.

'Lunch?' replied the hall porter in evident dismay. 'Lunch?'

'Yes,' I said, 'lunch. Isn't this a hotel?'

At this point my *sputnitsa*, faint but pursuing, took over. 'This,' she explained through a Georgian interpreter,

Tamara on and off the set

'A rather startled-looking family party'

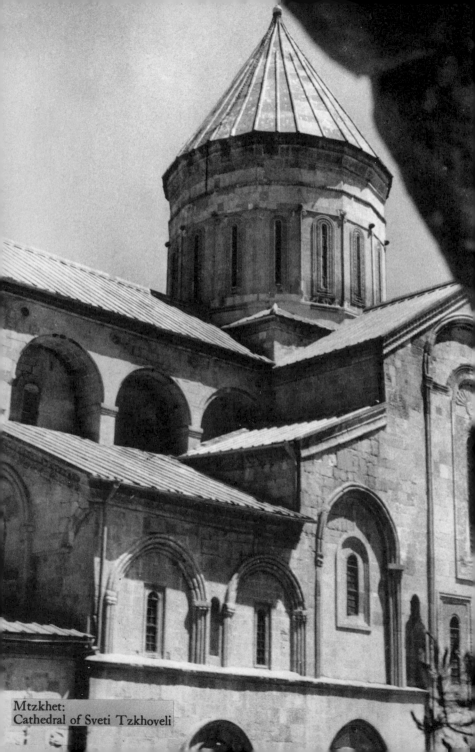

Mtzkhet:
Cathedral of Sveti Tzkhoveli

'is a foreign tourist who wants lunch.' There was a hasty confabulation in Russian and Georgian from which she emerged a minute or two later to say that we could have lunch. But not for an hour and a half. They had to go to the market to buy some food. Perhaps I would like to have another look at the museum and at Stalin's birthplace.

But no, I said, I had seen the museum and Stalin's birthplace. I would prefer simply to wait until luncheon was ready. And so I waited about hungrily for ninety minutes while the whole hotel was slowly put into working order, food was brought and the kitchen range was lighted, and, towards four in the afternoon, luncheon was eventually produced — no doubt the first luncheon to be served there since Khrushchov's speech of February 1956 had made it clear beyond a doubt that pilgrimages to Stalin's birthplace were no longer ideologically correct.

The sheep we had for luncheon at Gori may well have been a hill sheep. It had a sort of highland springiness about it which might well have derived from a youth spent in the foothills of the Caucasus. If so, it was the only hill sheep with which I came into contact during the whole of my month in the Soviet Union. At the collective farm which we took in on the way home there were no sheep, nothing but vineyards and cherry orchards. But the vineyards and the cherry orchards were all that they should be, especially those which the members of the collective farm cultivated on their own account, under the rule allowing each of them the right to farm an acre or so for himself and to sell the produce for what it will fetch on the open market. And so, after a drink of delicious newly made wine, we set off again for Tiflis, laden down with the cherries which our kind hosts had pressed upon us.

I was sorry when, a day or two later, the time came to leave Tiflis. On the other hand I was pleased to be travelling back to Moscow by train, for I had happy memories of pre-war train journeys in ancient railway carriages dating back to long before the Revolution and full of convivial fellow passengers. The de luxe class sleeping-compartment into which I climbed at Tiflis railway station was brand-new. But it had about it, like so many new things in the Soviet Union, an air of solid Victorian comfort, not to say luxury. There was an abundance of bronze and brass, of cut glass and polished mahogany. The curtains, which buttoned, were of thick red velvet. There was a Bokhara carpet on the floor. The radiator was hidden behind a heavy ornamental bronze grille. The railway being wide-gauge, the whole carriage was much wider and more spacious than a railway coach in Western Europe. At the end of the passage was a samovar, fired by charcoal, from which a motherly conductress dispensed endless glasses of hot sweet tea in little ornamental metal holders. For breakfast, which I had in bed, there were piping-hot *piroshki*, crisply fried golden brown savory beignets, brought round in a basket wrapped in a clean white napkin. The food in the restaurant car was excellent: borshch, smoked sturgeon, shashlik, Bœuf Stroganov, a wide range of excellent Georgian wines. Observing that I was reading *Anna Karenina* the head waiter, a portly man with a deep bass voice, at once

engaged me in conversation. Did I like Anna? he asked.
And what did I think of the way she behaved? And had
she been right to throw herself under the train? Did it
or did it not show a proper sense of responsibility? Our
discussion, animated but friendly, lasted on and off all
the way to Moscow.

During the daytime the de luxe passengers emerged
from their compartments and stood chatting in the corri-
dor: a major-general who had exchanged his much
bemedalled tunic for some brightly striped pyjamas, a
tremendously gracious lady of uncertain age, a couple of
Edwardian-looking children, and several Georgians who
all looked like Adolphe Menjou. My *sputnitsa*, for her
part, was by now completely exhausted and spent the day
prostrate on her bunk.

Had I heard, my travelling companions asked excitedly,
the result of the second football match between England
and the Soviet Union? It had been a draw again: 2 — 2.
And now we should have to wait for the third match to
see who really had the best team.

In the night the engine emitted not the cheerful toot
of an English train but the long drawn out wolflike wail
affected by locomotives in Russia and North America. It
reminded me of all the Russian train journeys I had ever
made.

We woke next morning to a steamy landscape of vineyards and tea plantations and wooded hills. Soon we had
reached the coast and were chugging past the famous
pleasure resorts of the Black Sea Riviera — Sukhum,
Gagri, Sochi — with their palm trees, their smart asphalted
promenades, and their dazzling white villas and hotels

147

set against a green background of subtropical vegetation. At one point we halted a few yards from the water's edge, and in a flash three-quarters of the passengers were out of the train and had all dived into the sea until finally the whistle blew and we scrambled moistly back into our compartments. My *sputnitsa*, I noticed with interest, had been wearing a smart polka-dotted bikini under her dress.

That night, as it was getting dark, we had our last view of the Caucasus, a line of remote snow-capped peaks on the horizon, far away across an endless expanse of green cornfields.

I was greeted immediately on my return to Moscow with the grim news of the execution in Hungary of Imre Nagy and General Pal Maleter. Amongst some foreign diplomats and journalists in the capital there was a tendency to interpret this tragic ending to a tragic story as betokening a radical change of policy on the part of the Kremlin, a sudden turn for the worse. To me it seemed no more than a salutary reminder of the continuing realities of the situation; a change of emphasis, at most the opening of a new tactical phase in the cold war.

Was it not, after all absolutely true to form? Was it not the logical conclusion of a process which had begun when the Red tanks rumbled into Budapest two years earlier? After massacring out of hand thousands of the rank and file of the Hungarian resistance why should the powers that be, whether Russian or Hungarian, spare the ringleaders, especially when those ringleaders possessed the added stigma of being renegade Party members, lapsed Communists, rabid revisionists? Was it not only natural that the rulers of the Soviet Empire, wishing at this particular moment to demonstrate their contempt for the West and their dislike for Tito, wishing at the same time to issue a warning to Premier Gomulka of Poland and perhaps also to pull up with a round turn any revisionists or near-revisionists there might be in the Soviet Union itself, should have seized on this convenient opportunity to rub out publicly, as a sharp object lesson to all concerned, a couple of top-ranking revisionists whom for the past two years they had been keeping on ice no doubt for this very purpose and this very moment? Surely, in the circumstances, it would have been in the highest degree unrealistic to expect bourgeois moral or humanitarian scruples to play a part in their calculations, less still concern for left-wing public opinion abroad, which in such matters has a notoriously short memory. No. If ever there was one, this was a reminder of the realities of the situation, of the situation as it was now and as it was likely to remain for a long time to come.

For in my view there is not at present likely to be any slacking off in the clash of conflicting ideologies, the battle of subversion, agitation and propaganda. On the contrary, it is likely if anything to be further intensified, to be fought by the Russians with greater skill and greater subtlety on a greater number of fronts. For, despite the many far-reaching changes of the last five years, the ultimate aim of Soviet policy still remains the same. Russia is still Russia and communism is still communism. Even though there may at present be no reign of terror, the basic ideological principles and assumptions which made possible the reign of terror are still there, ready to be applied should the circumstances demand it. In the Soviet mind facts are still distorted to fit theories. Unquenchable hostility to the whole of the non-communist world is still the foundation of Soviet policy. World revolution, or, to define it more closely, the ultimate extension of Soviet domination to the whole of the non-communist world, is still its aim — an aim which Khrushchov, or any other Communist worthy of the name, knows with the whole force of his Marxist faith, with the ineluctable force of historical determinism, is bound in the long run to be triumphantly attained.

On the question of how it will be attained it is interesting to note in passing that there has recently been a significant change of doctrine. In a pronouncement to the Twentieth Party Congress in February 1956, Mr Khrushchov formally threw overboard Lenin's dogma of the 'fatal inevitability of war' as a pre-condition of world revolution and enunciated in its place the entirely new theory that, owing to the rapid decline of capitalism and the strengthening of the forces of socialism, the millennium might well in the end be achieved by peaceful or semi-peaceful means.

Nor do I personally think that the Russians want a hot war. Certainly nothing could be further from the wishes of the Soviet people. They suffered appallingly in both the last two wars — a fact of which the foreign visitor to the Soviet Union is reminded at every turn and in every conversation. And though they would no doubt once again fight bravely were their country attacked they cannot possibly have any desire for war as such. Nor does it seem to me at all likely that the Soviet Government want a hot war either. Why should they, after all? They could, it is true, probably blot out the British Isles (a fact of which one is also more or less tactfully reminded on occasion). But that would do them very little good by comparison with the appalling and probably decisive damage which they themselves would inevitably suffer at the hands of the West. Far better, surely, from their point of view, to carry on with the cold war, which at the present moment seems to be going largely their way.

A gloomy prospect? Not a very cheerful one, perhaps — prospects seldom are cheerful nowadays. But to my mind much less gloomy, for either side, than that of mutual annihilation. A prospect, too, which at least offers scope for manœuvre and for a positive policy, if only one happens to have one.

Under Stalin, as Khrushchov has said, things in the Soviet Union were paralysed, frozen. Now, thanks partly to the course of events and partly to Khrushchov's own intervention, things are no longer paralysed; they are moving. The ice is breaking up.

The task which confronts Khrushchov himself is an extremely tricky one. He is trying to do something which very few people have ever succeeded in doing, least of all in Russia. He is trying, up to a point, to liberalize a tyranny, to replace a reign of terror by a rather milder form of government, to let a little fresh air into the Soviet Union from outside. And in Russia it has always been the tyrants, men of the type of Stalin and Ivan the Terrible, who have prospered and eventually died in their beds; while the reformers, the liberalizers, the tsars who granted constitutions, have usually come to a sticky end.

Khrushchov may well be lucky. He may well succeed in his task. He is, as I have said, a remarkably able and determined man who should on no account be under-estimated. But, whatever the outcome of his experiment, one thing seems to me reasonably certain: by the time he, or whoever takes over from him, has completed it, by the time he has carried out the operation which he claims will bring Soviet industrial and economic development level with that of the United States, in say fifteen or twenty years from now, there will inevitably have been far-reaching, fundamental changes in the character of the Soviet regime.

It is impossible, in such matters, to stop half-way. Having once granted a little freedom the rulers of the Soviet Union will be bound to grant more freedom. Having once improved the standard of living of the population they will have, in the long run, to improve it still further. Finally, having let in a little fresh air from outside they will have to let in more. Nothing in the Soviet Union struck me more forcibly than the hunger of every Soviet citizen I talked to for news of the outside world. They have been starved of it for so long that it has become an overwhelming obsession with them. And now that they have acquired the taste they will, in the long run, some-how find the means of satisfying it. Already it is extraordi-nary how many people in Moscow manage to listen to foreign broadcasts, to get hold of foreign books and papers and fashion-plates and gramophone records, and to talk to foreigners or to Russians who have been abroad.

And then there is the new aristocracy to be reckoned with — the new educated class, the new rich, the officers, the technocrats and the bureaucrats and their luxuriously brought up children, with their private cars, their *rok-i-rol* records, their champagne suppers and their skiffle groups. 'A generation is growing up who think differently from us,' said Khrushchov recently. And sure enough he has on his hands a new class, a rising class which is not entirely subordinated to the Party and which will not blindly accept the Party line, a class interested in their work and their jobs and their possessions and in having a good time and in their own vested interests, a tough class with few illusions which in the long run will become politically harder and harder to deal with. 'Why,' I said to one of them, 'do you think Khrushchov has had Nagy executed?' 'Oh,' he replied, without even bothering to look whether anyone was listening, 'probably because he thought it was a shame to keep an innocent man in prison any longer.' Coming from a Soviet citizen it was a startlingly cynical reply.

On the other hand we should not forget that, to help him in his task, Khrushchov has a number of very considerable assets. The average Soviet citizen, the average Russian especially, is patriotically inclined. He is also by now ideologically conditioned. He may be critical about points of detail, but he does not really question the fundamental rightness of the regime. He is curious about foreign countries but he is passionately attached to his own, to the actual soil of Russia. For most Russians Holy Russia, the Russian way of life, life shared hugger-mugger with millions and millions of other Russians, still has the same overwhelming powers of attraction it has always had.

Nor is this all. The average Soviet citizen, who has never been abroad, can only judge conditions in his country now by what things used to be like there in the past. He has never seen anything else. And by this standard of comparison he will see, as I myself saw, a very marked improvement over the past few years. He will come to feel that he has a vested interest in the continuance of the present regime. For this reason, provided the improvement in the standard of living keeps pace with the increase in individual liberty, it should be possible to avoid excessive discontent, to avoid the danger of any sudden explosion.

Indeed, in allowing increased contacts with the outside world, the Soviet Government may well calculate that before so very long they will no longer have anything to fear from free comparison with foreign countries. But by the time that that is so, the Soviet Union may well be an altogether different place, with a different standard of living, different standards of behaviour and a different kind of regime. In other words, by the time the Russians catch up with the Americans, the two countries, who already have a surprising amount in common, may well be practically indistinguishable. 'There are,' wrote Alexis de Tocqueville in 1835, with astonishing foresight, 'at the present time two great nations in the world, which started at different points, but seem to tend towards the same end. I mean the Russians and the Americans ... Each of them seems marked out by the will of Heaven to sway the destinies of half the globe.'

What conclusions should we in the West draw from all this? My own view is that the best, if not the only hope of peace for humanity lies in the gradual evolution of the Soviet regime into something easier to live with than what confronts us at present. It may be a slender hope, but it is the best we have. I consider, therefore, that while vigorously keeping our own end up, we should do anything we conveniently can to hurry on the process of evolution, and help to let all the fresh air we can into the Soviet Union. The Soviet Government, for their part, are prepared to allow foreigners to visit their country. They are even prepared to allow a few Soviet citizens to travel abroad. To my mind we should take full advantage of this. The more contacts, the more exchanges of visits that take place, both official and unofficial, the better. We certainly have nothing to fear from them or from any comparisons which may be drawn between our two systems. On the contrary there is from our point of view every advantage that as many Russians as possible should see for themselves what the West is really like, and that as many Westerners as possible should see what Russia really is like. Personally, I have sufficient faith in the superiority of our system and of the ideas that lie behind it to say that this can do nothing but good.

It is, of course, quite possible that Khrushchov's confidence may turn out to be justified, and that as a result of his policy of relaxing pressure internally and allowing increased contacts with the outside world the rate of Soviet economic and technical development may be greatly increased. But though this may mean that we have to face fiercer economic competition, I do not believe that it would necessarily be to our disadvantage. And that for one very good reason: the more say the Russian people have in their own affairs, and the happier and more prosperous they become, the less likely are they to allow themselves to become involved in war. For us the important thing, to my mind, is to hold our own in the cold war, for the next fifteen or twenty years, to hold it politically, economically and militarily. If we can do that, and if the world during that period can avoid a hot war, it may well be that the worst of our troubles will be over.

Strachur, May 1959